Kaizen

Japanese Techniques, Strategies, and Techniques
Using the Theories and Principles of Kaizen and
Ikigai

LIAM KEPLERS

Contents

Chapter One

Introduction

Applying philosophy to business has long been a leading trend in Japan. This was done in an effort to encourage people to start viewing business as a significant force in our society rather than just a way for corporations to make money. The kaizen philosophy gained notoriety in the 1980s when several Japanese businesses began to employ it in order to make small improvements that ultimately helped them to dominate the entire world in terms of output, profits, and employee satisfaction.

The holistic approach of kaizen teaches us to pay attention to the little things in life and to concentrate on them. It does away with the necessity of having lofty objectives and goals in favor of emphasizing the value of daily improvements that can be made gradually.

It maintains that nothing cannot be improved upon and that therefore everything must be improved, making it a never-ending process. This zeal is part of what makes Kaizen what it is. It spurs management to create better policies, identify areas for improvement, and completely transform how the business operates while motivating employees.

Kaizen's exclusivity comes from the fact that it involves every aspect of the business and does not hold upper management and employees to be inherently different from one another. Instead, it emphasizes the significance of each component of work, and there is a reason for this. Workers are the ones who use the machinery and perform all of the labor. Kaizen forces management to consider employee input so that their skills and knowledge can be used to identify areas for improvement.

In this book, we'll discuss the various Kaizen strategies, including the 5S, the TPS (Toyota Production System), the 5M's, the Lean Production System, and others. We'll also discuss how to implement Kaizen into your company through training and holding Kaizen events.

There is also a section that is dedicated to applying Kaizen to startups. Finally, we'll talk about how Kaizen can help you in your personal life and what uses it has outside of the business world.

In addition to Kaizen, there are other Japanese philosophies that can serve as life guidelines, such as Ikigai, which encourages people to find their purpose in life. We will also go into great detail about this theory and its tenets.

Chapter Two

Foundations of Kaizen

To understand Kaizen, we must first examine its origins and the factors that contributed to its success. About thirty years ago, Masaaki Imai popularized the business philosophy known as Kaizen. He wrote a book that codified the concept into the canon of business management and established it as a social norm in the larger mainstream culture. It's a phrase with its roots primarily in business, but you can use it to change your habits in everyday life.

It is a Japanese word whose meaning can be determined by dividing it. Kai denotes change, while Zen denotes striving for betterment. This phrase can be translated as "improvement" when these words are used together.

Despite having its historical roots in Japan, Kaizen's manufacturing and commercial potential could only truly be realized in America. Because they lacked the resources or the time to implement drastic changes that would have increased production during World War II, American manufacturers were forced to rely on making small adjustments to their regular working environment to achieve better results. As the workers became accustomed to the daily changes brought on by these small ones, they began to perform better and adapt to the changes. Following its formalization, this method is now used by almost all organizations.

The manufacturing company Toyota, which in 2001 published a book on its manufacturing ideals and stressed the significance of incremental change in its work process, is credited with popularizing Kaizen.

Then what is Kaizen? It is a strategy that emphasizes daily improvement over the bigger picture and the eventual revolutionization of commerce and daily routines. In order to succeed, Kaizen maintains that we must constantly improve. This philosophy holds that larger goals would be achieved automatically if small changes were made every day.

The psychology behind this is fascinating because whenever you set yourself a goal, you always have a tendency to think beyond what is actually feasible. We all like to set goals and objectives that are as big as they can be, but constantly thinking about how to accomplish them can have a negative impact on your mind. Because the task we have set for ourselves is so large and would require so much effort to complete, this discourages us from working. Due to this, only a select few people are able to take on and complete such tasks, while the majority simply give up.

Because it encourages you to enjoy the journey rather than place your attention on the end result, kaizen is unique. It wouldn't be any fun at all, and you wouldn't learn anything, if you simply achieved your goal in a single instant, as most people imagine after daydreaming about it. You'll be more motivated to complete your tasks if you divide the task into smaller, more manageable chunks and see improvements in yourself as a result. A change like this occurs every day, making it possible to observe it and learn from it, making it priceless. Additionally, Kaizen alters the way we think about achieving our goals. Rather than assuming that change can only come about through perseverance and taking big steps, it teaches us that life is made up of the little steps we take every day.

A man can climb a mountain by making small daily progress, but he can only succeed if he doesn't rush it and become exhausted. It takes more than just gazing up a mountain in the hopes of reaching the top and then sobbing in agony when you realize it's still a ways off to climb a mountain. If you ignore it and concentrate on each step you take, you will have a much greater chance of reaching the peak. You'll soon come to appreciate how enjoyable each step can be, and once you begin to concentrate on those minute details, work will seem much more manageable and enjoyable.

Imagine a worker who has been told by his team that he must finish a specific task by the end of the year regardless of the circumstances. He has the information necessary to complete this. He will begin to consider all the additional work he must do and how challenging it is to achieve his goal once he takes the first step toward achieving it. He won't be motivated to work on the task at hand if he hears this. Additionally, he will be less productive and less able to concentrate due to the stress of the bigger task, which will affect the work's quality. He would have been content to devote all of his attention and willpower to the task at hand, improving the outcomes for the company, had he only been concerned with the immediate task at hand and not worried about bigger goals.

By examining what has already been accomplished and taking pride in the

knowledge that at least a portion of the goal
has been achieved, our brain also encourages
us to be motivated. However, if we are only
concerned with the bigger picture, our brain
will never be satisfied. As a result, rather
than spurring us on to work harder, small
victories end up discouraging us because we
are constantly reminded of how insignificant
the task we just finished is in comparison to the
herculean one that needs to be accomplished.
Kaizen advises viewing each small task as
the entire goal in and of itself. By doing
this, every small task is perceived as a major
accomplishment, which keeps your brain
motivated. Your self-esteem will significantly
increase if you repeat this every day.

Kaizen makes sure you have a goal to work
toward every day and that you can come
to the end of each day knowing that you
made a small improvement. Any company's

ability to succeed depends on its employees, and the company can only grow when the employees do. As a result, Kaizen helps you concentrate on what is in front of you.

It encourages motivation and self-assurance, which ultimately boosts output and results in the accomplishment of the main objective.

Chapter Three

Center of Kaizen

The core of Kaizen is based on five guiding principles:

Recognize your customers

Just let it go

Enter Gemba

Enable people Maintain openness.

Continuous improvement can occur within the organization when all five of these principles are applied consistently.

Understand your customer

The customer is the starting point for everything in Kaizen. You will succeed if you have the ability to capture your customer's imagination and produce precisely what they require. Finding out what customers want and ensuring that they improve their experience by offering them satisfying products is the goal of any organization. How well a company creates value for its customers can be used to assess how well a business has improved through Kaizen.

Make it Flow

Zero waste development within the organization is another focus of kaizen. It regards everything as valuable and blames waste for the company's failure. When daily goals are established using the Kaizen system, the top priority is to make sure that nothing is wasted and that the most value is being extracted from every source that can be used.

Enter Gemba

The gemba, often referred to as the household, is where all actions take place. At the end of the day, all managers are required to abide by this rule. To see what's happening for yourself, you need to be connected to the areas where labor is generating value.

Develop People

Without everyone being aware of the necessary steps, kaizen cannot function. Without effective teamwork and communication, some members of the group won't be able to complete the task at hand and may instead choose to concentrate on the bigger picture rather than the more manageable steps. When people trust one another and can freely communicate, everyone in the organization is aware of their responsibilities.

Be Open-Book

Kaizen cannot succeed unless participants can personally witness the bigger objectives that are accomplished at the end of the year. Without first assessing how the results are affecting the organization's overall productivity, you can't just keep making haphazard improvements. Management must therefore make sure that they have the appropriate data and that they regularly publish it for public consumption.

PDAC Cycle

The PDCA cycle must be continuously run in order to achieve kaizen. It refers to the Plan-Do-Check-Act cycle, also referred to as the Deming cycle. Every person who is working will have an attitude that encourages them to aim for higher levels of productivity thanks to this cycle. This cycle makes sure that there is continuous improvement in the work's quality and quantity while also lowering costs at every stage. It basically means that bigger improvements in the organization can only occur if we constantly review the work cycle to raise the standard, cut down on waste, and maximize the use of the resources we do have. When Kaizen is used in conjunction with this cycle, everyone eventually begins to cooperate in a way that allows all production processes to be carefully examined in order to maximize productivity.

Plan

Planning everything out properly is the first step in the entire process. You must choose the company's production strategy, including what and how you are producing it. This theme is crucial because it outlines for your staff how work should proceed and what tasks they should complete. Everyone is able to comprehend the production process and keep an eye out for issues as a result. Study the company's material and financial situation after that, and then think of creative ways to complete tasks. Establish the tasks that need to be completed, identify the problem areas, analyze these problem areas to determine the cause of the chaos, and then begin developing solutions to fix the issues.

Do

Finding out what needs to be done comes after you have completed all of the analysis. Then make a list of the actions that need to be taken for increased productivity across the entire organization.

Chapter Four

Background of Kaizen

Through the works of Masaaki Imai, the term "Kaizen" itself received widespread acclaim. Masaaki Imai is a Japanese managerial scholar and board expert who specializes in Kaizen and is known for his work on quality control. He was born in 1930. The Kaizen Institute Consulting Group (KICG) was established in 1985 to help western organizations comprehend Kaizen's concepts and how they can be applied in various cultural contexts.

Kaizen was established in a number of Japanese businesses that had, in one way or another, incorporated American and even European leadership techniques and competencies. A select group of significant businesses, who are in charge of fostering efficiency and raising productivity, oversaw the development of these strategies.

Kaizen was first used by Japanese businesses during World War II, who were the first to incorporate the philosophy into their manufacturing. Using this method, they implemented efficient production cycles. This had been influenced by American business and quality management educators who had visited the nation to some extent. Because of its effectiveness, all contemporary businesses now employ this revolutionary idea that became extremely well-liked in Japan in the 1950s.

Japan's products were regarded as reasonably priced but of rather lower quality during the period of economic reconstruction following World War II. The Union of Japanese Scientists and Engineers was among the organizations that played a significant role in that film as part of the effort to increase quality and efficiency in order to counteract this type of negative publicity (JUSE). For large corporations as well as occasionally executives, they conducted a number of educational workshops on statistical management techniques and even quality assurance. Through these programs, businesses began to appreciate the importance of quality control and to put forth effort to set up manufacturing facilities of the highest caliber. For a variety of workplace improvement tasks, such as waste management (Muda-Dori), cost reduction, industrial safety management, defect reduction, 5S (which we will cover later), and creation of quality circles, voluntary organizations were established in each stage of development. A quality circle is a group of employees who perform the same or comparable roles and who meet on a regular basis to comprehend, assess, and take responsibility for issues pertaining to the workplace. The PDCA Cycle is the same as a quality circle, but workers rather than management complete it.

Organizations representing businesses, academia, and labor unions founded the JPC (Japan Productivity Center) in 1955. While becoming a successful national organization, JPC led the growth campaign. Since 1955, the JPC has dispatched numerous missions to numerous contemporary manufacturing facilities in developed nations, including the U.S., to observe their productivity and technological advancements. The obtained results were discussed at feedback sessions held across the nation, and they were also compiled for distribution to interested businesses. This strategy contributed to the overall rise in quality and efficiency of Japanese businesses.

A large number of Japanese businesses launched several initiatives to help boost efficiency and performance as a form of effective business strategy by working extremely hard on the quality of their goods from the combined point of view of manufacturing, producing, and maintaining good products and services. At this point, the Total Quality Control (TQC) concept was born. High-profile Japanese businesses like Yamaha, Sony, Honda, Canon, Nissan, Panasonic, Toyota, and Suzuki persistently promoted the use of Total Quality Control throughout the country. That is what has made them global leaders in efficient manufacturing and development.

These measures were institutionalized and their reach was increased by numerous public and private sectors. Soon, these strategies were not only used in the manufacturing industry, but also to increase client loyalty. Some American and European corporate executives, academics, and engineers who traveled to Japan to study the key components of Japanese companies' capacity to improve their businesses focused on the Kaizen modification. Several companies then imported Japanese production and manufacturing management know-how and reorganized it to fit the American and European business environments.

As previously stated, the quality and manufacturing techniques were initially introduced from the United States to Japan. Over time, Japanese producers changed and improved the techniques based on their various sizes, markets, production environments, and other relevant factors.

TPS

The Toyota Production System (TPS) is a well-known and reputable management system. TPS is built around two key ideas: Jidoka and Just-In-Time. To prevent the production of defective goods, the Jidoka is used to immediately shut down a malfunctioning system. The Just-In-Time method, on the other hand, is based on only producing as many goods as are required to prevent producing excess goods. Likewise, make sure there are enough raw materials in storage to guarantee a smooth manufacturing process.

To elaborate further, the fundamental tenets upon which TPS is built are as follows:

Jidoka Jidoka focuses on illuminating and visualizing problems so that they are not suppressed but are instead made clear to everyone, enabling problems to be quickly fixed. It is predicated on the notion that a product's value and the value of the entire company depend on how manufacturing is carried out. For instance, if a defective part is discovered or a piece of equipment breaks down, the damaged unit will immediately stop operating, requiring the operators to halt production while they address and resolve the issue.

What does that imply? This indicates that the system shuts down until regular operations can be resumed. This guarantees that, in the event of an equipment malfunction or a service issue, the machines will stop automatically, isolate the issue, and only resume production of goods in accordance with the company's quality standards. The visual notice boards are used to communicate problems because the system automatically stops when one arises (ondon). This makes it easier for operators to keep looking into other systems and to identify anything that might have caused the problem right away in order to stop it from happening again.

This entails that multiple operators will be in charge of as many machines as there are in the company, resulting in improved efficiency while also allowing for constant, limitless changes, leading to increased production power.

Just-in-Time

To improve quality, use this technique. It permits the production of only the goods that are deemed necessary and in the required quantities. Through Jidoka, all components made and supplied must adhere to the appropriate quality standards already established by the manufacturer. The effectiveness of this particular approach to the development of high-quality products lies in its ability to increase profits while completely eliminating waste, irrational demands on the production line, and even inconsistencies. For instance, if a customer wants their new car when they want it, it must be manufactured efficiently as and when it is needed. This means that manufacturing needs to be extremely effective and efficient in order to occur quickly.

Kaizen is an overarching philosophy that encourages the continual improvement of an organization's operations, according to Masaki Imai. Since any company's current system is constantly being questioned, it is frequently said that the task of change is never complete.

How did this tactic get so popular? After Toyota used it to take control of the automotive industry, it gained popularity. Employees at Toyota were encouraged to see the company's challenges, no matter how small they might seem, rather than just pursuing big endeavors. They had access to the best solutions and were allowed to map the problems' origins.

Two strategies are frequently employed by Japanese industrial businesses. These are the bottom-up approach under the Quality Control Process, led by a community group, and the empirical method, which is centered on data processing. First, this is done to make sure that no information about the company is being withheld. Every issue must be exposed and fixed as soon as possible. The bottom-up strategy makes sure that the employees care about what they're doing, which encourages careful work rather than carelessness that could result in manufacturing flaws. The main reason Japanese businesses are successful is because they treat their employees with respect, pay them a living wage, and provide them with a compelling reason to care about their work. People, not machinery, make up the entire organization.

Japan is now known as the "nation of world quality" due to the extensive quality and efficiency enhancement initiatives undertaken by a large number of Japanese businesses, whose production levels have improved from subpar to outstanding.

Let's take an example: in 1990, a study team from the Massachusetts Institute of Technology (MIT) examined the Toyota Production Process in order to pinpoint potential sources of competitive advantage for the Japanese auto industry. They then published a book titled "The Machine Changing the World" as a result of their research. Throughout this book, TPS was developed upon, rearranged, and finally given the name "Lean Manufacturing System." These researchers continued to criticize this system because they thought a top-down strategy would be preferable to a bottom-up strategy.

The General Electric (GE) Company eventually made it even better. The entire production system has now been integrated with the Kaizen system to guarantee process improvement throughout. The "Six Sigma" and the "Lean and Six Sigma," which were later combined to form "Lean and Six Sigma," have been integrated with Kaizen and have emerged as contemporary examples of western productivity and product development.

The central tenet of Kaizen is that those who perform all roles in the company are the ones who know their jobs best; by showing confidence in their abilities, project management is enhanced to a greater extent than was initially possible. Every wall has to start dissolving for more effective progress to occur, and this particular collaborative project encourages creativity and transition, both of which include every tier of workers. Kaizen is a way of life, not just a strategy for increasing the profitability of the manufacturing sector. Everyone has an interest in change, which explains this. Kaizen helps everyone's job become easier by breaking down problems into their component parts, analyzing each one, and making changes as needed. Since everyone in the organization is a member and thus has a role to play, kaizen cannot be limited to just one person and must involve everyone. Kaizen must for each individual become a strategy of continuous improvement for them as well as the business.

Masaki Imai asserts that there are three main pillars of Kaizen. He stated that in order to meet the fundamental standards, management and employees must be able to cooperate. He identifies the visual administration, the leader's position within the organization, and the growth of a business that depends on training and experience as the three main factors that must be taken into account for this to be effective.

Chapter Five

The Upkeep of Kaizen's Pillars

In Japanese, the term "Gemba" refers to the workplace. The transformative process of managing the workplace is the main focus of this approach. A place called the Gemba was created so that value could be added to both the product and the service it offers before they were transferred to the following production cycle. An engineering framework was employed to achieve this. The 5S is their name.

This was taken from the first characters of the five words in Japanese. There are five requirements for a secure and healthy working environment. The 5S stand for organization, purity, discipline, strictness, and cleanliness, respectively (tidiness).

To arrange, straighten out, sweep, sanitize, and maintain the workplace is a succinct way to translate them into English. The 5S helps reveal information about how organized a workplace is. Cleaning, health, and ergonomic standards must be adhered to by both manufacturing and non-manufacturing organizations. In order to implement The Five S, employees' opinions about a company's manufacturing division, the entire business, and even one another, must be examined. For any manufacturing organization, this is now a crucial resource. Manufacturing businesses can become world-class thanks to the 5S strategy.

The 5S

They are:

Seiri

Finding out what is necessary from what is not is known as seiri. Things that you don't think are important can be tagged using the red tag method. Prior to being discarded, everyone should be able to decide whether the products are needed or not. Red-tagged items need to be sold, given away, sold to staff, trashed, or given to scrap dealers.

Seiton

The purpose of Seiton is to draw attention to the items that require preservation and protection. This serves to bring those things into view. To make it simple to identify materials by their location, they should be labeled and highlighted. Everything has its proper place according to the law, so employees should have an idea of where these spaces are located.

Seiso

Seiso translates to cleaning up whatever is left. Making sure they are clean and, if possible, painting them to give them a more enticing appearance.

Seiketsu

Seiketsu involves testing and disseminating information every day. Everyone wants to be informed about changes that occur in some of the company's chosen Kaizen areas. They should receive the necessary training, and you should make sure that everyone has access to the information they need regarding these changes.

Shitsuke

Standardization and self-discipline are key concepts in Shitsuke. First, plan a reasonably smooth schedule, and make sure to tidy up and organize your workspace during downtime.

Additional advantages of the 5S include:

creating environments that are safe, friendly, and healthy for workers

The workforce is revitalized, and productivity and morale among employees are raised.

eliminates the need to look for the necessary instruments, saving time. Because of this, the operators' job is very simple.

Along with clearing up the workspace, it aids in reducing taxing work.

As a result of the shared solidarity and sense of belonging it fosters among the workforce, the employees experience a sense of belonging to a caring community.

disposal of waste

Muda is the Japanese word for waste. Wastes are items that don't add value to the workplace. Work is defined as a sequence of tasks that improve the product. There are a variety of items, such as components of the finished product or even raw materials, that don't add value but instead cause more issues. Here are a few examples of waste produced by businesses:

faulty parts, excess inventory, unnecessary transportation of components, and production-delaying inspections are some examples of overproduction.

All of these activities are regarded as office waste, including document routing, pointless paperwork and certificate signing, workers receiving a ton of papers and files that bury them, pointless data, and the transmission of work that contains errors.

There are seven deadly wastes.

Overproduction

This happens when equipment malfunctions, employee disengagement, and rejection take place. Trying to outpace production at other times can result in significant waste. In addition, it results in a wasteful use of utilities and human resources, higher interest costs, the consumption of raw materials before they are needed, high administrative and transportation costs, a greater need for space than is necessary for the storage of excess inventory, etc.

Motion

A waste is any kind of staff movement that does not improve the output. Because it is risky, challenging, and a sign of non-value-adding activities, the staff should refrain from lifting or carrying objects that call for a lot of force or effort. To reduce needless human movement, rearranging the workspace would be extremely helpful.

Deficiencies

Duplication of time and money is perfectly illustrated by manufacturing halts, rejected products, and their subsequent replication. These rejections can increase the amount of paperwork that needs to be completed, as well as the amount of time needed for inspection, repair, and employee availability to stop the machines when instructed.

Waiting

In the event that the operators are idle, this occurs. This is known as waiting because it wastes time when an operator's task is delayed due to downtime or a lack of small parts. When a product is manufactured, the lead time begins when the company purchases the raw materials needed to make it and ends when it receives payment from customers for the product in question. Cash turnover is governed by Lead Time. The shorter the lead time, the more effectively resources are being used, the more adaptable the company is in meeting customer demands, and the less money is being spent on operations. Waste management is a crucial tool in Kaizen. Other types of waste in this category include things, products, documents, and information that are unused, add nothing to the production process, and yet cost the business money to maintain.

Chapter Six

Kaizen and Business

You can use Kaizen to launch and grow your own business, which is another important goal. A business doesn't just appear out of nowhere. Neither did Rome. And even once your business is up and running, you'll still need to make small improvements in order to build your brand and keep growing. This is why Kaizen emphasizes "gradual progression" because it is designed to make sure that businesses endure.

Ever had the desire to start a business? Why didn't you just go ahead and do that? Is it as a result of your current obligations to your family, your day job, or other activities in your life taking up all of your time? Nobody is born to be a businessman. However, what steps should you take to make it happen if you think this path might be right for you?

Think of this: Pick an appropriate time each day to sit down and visualize the future of your company. Let's take a moment to imagine ourselves as businessmen. Identify your goals by asking yourself the following questions. Where do you plan to sell it? How many staff members would you need to hire? Where are suppliers likely to be found?

The exercise will accomplish two things:

Now that you're more committed to starting the business you've always wanted,

You'll start using your imagination to look for the solutions and gather the necessary resources.

Keep in mind that with Kaizen, our intention is to acclimate you gradually to this ground-breaking methodology: a little bit every day can result in more significant changes. As a result, consider the most practical action or measures that could bring about your vision:

Give yourself an hour a day to explore the sector you're thinking about starting.

One person who already works in your industry might be able to help you establish your business, so try to interview one person per day who does.

Meet other businessmen who share your viewpoints and ask them what they think of your idea for a company and how they managed to succeed.

You don't have to leave your current job before you're ready to launch your own business. Small acts are still perfectly possible even if you are currently working professionally elsewhere. How complex your financial plan is will ultimately determine how quickly you succeed. Always keep in mind that with Kaizen, every concept can be broken down into smaller concepts. Making small, steady progress (weekly or monthly) toward your goal, which enables you to take everything in stride rather than at a run, is the main reason, of course, why it's a successful philosophy. No matter what rate of growth you want for your company, it will ultimately be fueled by this consistent continuity.

expanding your business

An attitude of Kaizen is advantageous if you already run a business or hold a supervisory position. If you can put the Kaizen theory into practice at home and at work, this is ideal. However, in order to fully implement Kaizen into your business, your staff must also be on board. Here are some recommendations for developing a "Kaizen working environment":

View the Important Business Practices

Start by identifying the business sectors that are crucial to the success of your company. Manufacturing, purchasing, selling, and providing client assistance are a few examples of such activities. Then, each month, make an effort to get the staff to concentrate on one significant goal for each of the company's branches. Such a statement might go like this: "This quarter, we're going to increase our clientele by at least 10%." Your manufacturing capacity, customer service, and marketing requirements may all be improved as a result of this goal. Last but not least, you need to create an annual goal for the growth of your business that involves every division.

Look for Daily Activities

Find three daily tasks that your sales team should consistently complete to achieve this goal. You might advise them to do the following, for instance, to increase the firm's market share:

Every day, contact five satisfied current customers and request their help in identifying any additional people who might be interested in our product.

Send current subscribers an email update informing them of the most recent updates we can provide this quarter.

To help people understand and learn about our service innovations, publish one new blog update on the company website every day.

Naturally, the actions you choose depend on your own situation. However, the goal is to have everyone in the company regularly working on the most crucial projects and hitting the monthly goals. These consistent, gradual actions motivated by Kaizen help the staff stay on task each morning and keep them from forgetting what's crucial for a productive work shift.

Developing a Stronger Sense of Community Through Kaizen

The team is able to perform at a higher level of effectiveness when it feels motivated. If an employee participates in the processes of the company, they are more likely to be receptive to new suggestions that are beneficial to the company. Employees are able to feel a sense of connection to their job, company, peers, and work when they have a strong sense of team spirit because it is a sense of unity that they share. People are able to experience a sense of fulfillment as a result of feeling as though they are a part of something bigger than themselves. People have a tendency to perform their jobs more effectively when they are satisfied with their lives. They become less self-centered as a result, as they begin to assist others with their work or take on additional responsibilities in order to see the success of the company.

If you want employees who are dedicated to their work, you need to work on building team spirit. Nevertheless, you won't be able to successfully build team spirit by simply taking all of your employees out to lunch once every few days. It is necessary to convince them that they are all the same and think in the same way. Acquire some matching t-shirts, cups, and other items that serve as a constant reminder to them that they are a part of the team in order to foster a feeling of cohesiveness among the members of the group. Give people mementos that remind them of the team they're a part of, and you'll keep their team spirit alive. Our feelings are represented by the things we own, and through them we construct meaning for ourselves.

You are going to have to come to terms with the fact that you cannot manage your employees. You have no choice but to instruct them in the desired behavior, equip them with the resources necessary to carry it out, and cross your fingers that they are successful. When you try to constantly dictate what your employees should be doing, it can lead to frustration, anger, and a loss of motivation on their part. Employees will get the impression that you trust them more when you grant their requests to do what they want to do. One of the most effective ways to motivate most people is to give them opportunities to test themselves. They are much more likely to push themselves to demonstrate that they are worthy of your trust if you show that you have confidence in their abilities and then give them space to work things out on their own.

The following are three examples of Kaizen acts that can be used to inspire the team:

On a regular, monthly, or weekly basis, you should assign tasks (which each member of the team is required to complete) as follows: Give every employee the opportunity to inquire about, and provide an honest response to, "why" they have been given their particular tasks. The fact that they are responsible for those responsibilities should make them feel respected and empowered.

Do not just hand over responsibility to someone else without any kind of prior planning or preparation. Prepare the members of your group as well as your employees by organizing the appropriate training and preparation. Even a brief and consistent training period is enough to adequately prepare workers for the responsibilities they have.

The very last stage is always the most important one. Only by correlating the desirable positive behavior you want to see with a reward system is it possible to ensure a gradual but steady increase in worker productivity. Be aware that you are not terminating the employment of workers who are performing poorly. You are merely motivating your employees to achieve greater results and rewarding those who do an exceptional job.

However, there should not be a financial benefit to anyone. Research that was funded by the Federal Reserve found that offering monetary incentives to workers resulted in an unexpected decrease in their efficiency. This was due to the fact that workers began to view their work solely in terms of the amount of money they could make from it. Make use of alternative approaches instead to satisfy the employees' emotional requirements. The best method for motivating people is to show them appreciation and give them rewards. The vast majority of people do not have faith in themselves, and as a result, they rely on the approval of others to make them feel as though they have value. A great number of individuals yearn for this kind of validation from influential people whose words, in comparison to their own, carry a great deal more weight. You can create an incentive system that will push people to work harder by showing appreciation and giving them rewards to the individuals who contribute to the system. Both of these things also add a touch of competition into the dynamic that exists between different employees. Your employees will find that this competition, so long as it is kept in a healthy spirit, serves as an excellent motivator for them.

Medals, certifications, or even perks could be used as a form of appreciation when good work is done that goes above and beyond what is expected. When you do give such memorabilia to people, it is important to remember to mention the specific act, their name, and everything else that individualizes the accomplishment for them. They should have the sense that they are seen and heard, and you shouldn't just give things like that away to everyone; in order to motivate people to work for it, a scarce commodity should be presented as an option.

Make sure that you acknowledge and reward good work within the working community by celebrating all successes as a team together and making sure that this happens. To ensure that the team is happy, as well as to make sure that they feel respected and humane, it is important to recognize work anniversaries, individual milestones, and even personal events such as birthdays, etc.

Kaizen Event

Improvement is the sole focus of a Kaizen event, which is organized and carried out by a business. This is a brief occurrence that normally only lasts for a couple of days at most.

The reason why it is referred to as an event is because it is necessary for every employee at the company to take part in it and gain knowledge about Kaizen. Not only does it instruct the employees of the company about Kaizen and how they can implement it, but it also serves as a kind of survey that looks into the functioning of the business in order to find areas in which there is room for improvement. The goal of a Kaizen event is to establish a foundation for the remaining months of the year. This is in contrast to the philosophy of Kaizen, which places an emphasis on making incremental improvements on a daily basis. After a Kaizen event has taken place, everyone is instructed on what they need to do and what they need to concentrate on, while at the same time any potential questions are answered. In this way, Kaizen can be incorporated into the workings of the company, and every day after the event, small gradual steps can be taken to improve the productivity of the company.

It is typically carried out by highly-trained Kaizen specialists that an organization is expected to employ. Due to the fact that this is a group endeavor, the organization is required to form a Kaizen team, which is then instructed by independent consultants from the outside. After the event is over, this Kaizen team will be able to take control of the situation and make certain that everyone is putting into practice the information they were instructed on during the course of the event itself.

After a Kaizen event has been carried out at a company, the majority of businesses have a tendency to forget about it and stop caring about it. This is a poor tactic due to the fact that any progress made during the competition will be lost immediately after it has concluded and will not be carried over into the subsequent months of the year. You need to make sure that your team takes Kaizen seriously if you want the benefits that you can receive from Kaizen to last for an extended period of time. It won't take long for the gains to be erased if the workers go back to doing things the way they always have, which means that you've just thrown away a fantastic opportunity.

By teaching the workers about the various programs that fall under Kaizen, the event itself has the potential to lead to a significant increase in the company's overall efficiency and productivity. For instance, the event itself has the potential to increase your profit margins by almost thirty to forty percent. This can be accomplished by teaching employees how to reduce waste. However, in order for this to work, it is necessary for you to ensure that the workforce is willing to listen and is receptive to the changes they are being asked to make. If you don't do this, the workforce will simply listen to the advice that the Kaizen trainers give them and then ignore it. You can even have your sales team and service team take a few sessions with Kaizen trainers so that they can learn to tackle their problems using the Kaizen approach of dividing everything into smaller components. A Kaizen event should also focus on areas other than just manufacturing.

To successfully carry out a Kaizen event, you will need to follow these steps in order:

Hire or Train Kaizen Leaders

For the event to be successful, you need someone who can take charge of it and run it smoothly. The trainer for a Kaizen program needs to be someone who can persuade the employees to buy into the Kaizen philosophy, just like they would for any other management technique. In addition to that, it needs to be someone who is experienced in the field. Find someone who is familiar with the lean philosophy and can explain how the Kaizen process functions. If you do not have the funds necessary to hire someone, you can simply begin conducting the Kaizen event on your own by reading up on the topic.

Acquire the confidence of the Senior Management Team.

If you want the changes that you are making to the organizational structure of the company to be successful, you need to make sure that the top management is on board with the changes. This indicates that you need to educate them about the significance of Kaizen and the reasons why they should also make it a priority in their lives to practice it.

Develop a strategy for the upcoming match.

You have to begin by defining the parameters of the event first. You need to have a clear understanding of which aspects of your work you want to apply the Kaizen methodology to. Are we only talking about the production floor, or does that encompass the office as well? Do you wish for the secretaries to acquire an understanding of Kaizen as well? The parameters of the event will be determined, in part, by your requirements. If you believe that there is a section of the business that has been both unprofitable and out of control, then you need to make sure that it is incorporated into the Kaizen event. The participation of each and every person in the Kaizen workshops is of the utmost importance and must be ensured. Because of this, the upper management needs to know what is being communicated to the manufacturing workers. This will allow them to understand how Kaizen can contribute to an increase in profits and what particular policies need to be adhered to in order to accomplish this goal.

You are also going to be responsible for establishing the purpose statement for the event. What exactly is it that you want to implement within your business? Do you plan on providing your employees with training on the 5S method? Or do you simply want them to constantly look for ways in which they can improve? When it comes to implementing Kaizen into the working environment, you and your team need to be able to communicate well with one another. You have to keep in mind that the majority of your employees may have never heard of Kaizen to begin with, and if you confuse them even more, they are not going to be particularly enthusiastic about performing the tasks that you want them to perform. You must remember this.

The only way for a Kaizen event to be successful is for everyone to be enthusiastic about the possibility of adopting this new philosophy. You want your employees to begin implementing Kaizen in their personal lives in addition to at work. Since its inception, Kaizen has served to instill within its participants the knowledge that they are capable of overcoming any challenge so long as they break it down into more manageable chunks.

Kaizen Training

The goal of the Kaizen Training is to educate every member of the organization about the system and get them ready to implement the small changes that they will be expected to make on a daily basis. It all begins with the top managers of the company; they are the ones who are tasked with learning why kaizen is so important and how it foresees their place in the company so that they can understand what it means. Kaizen will eventually evolve into a philosophy, and the only way it can be implemented successfully is if everyone is inspired by the potential it holds.

Chapter Seven

Top Management Training Top Management Attitude

It is necessary for the most important members of the upper executives to have a profound dedication to the Kaizen cause and to be excellent leaders in order for the Kaizen operations to make forward progress. If results are demanded immediately after implementing Kaizen without actually participating in any of its operations, employee morale will not improve; rather, horrible results will be produced, which will lead to even more problems. In order for Kaizen to be successfully implemented, the top managers are required to be able to communicate the most important aspects of the process through their actions. The fundamental questions that they need to answer for every member of the workforce are: What is Kaizen? What is the difference between creativity and Kaizen? What advantages does Kaizen have? How should the outcomes of Kaizen be measured, and what methods are required? Which methods and procedures are available for putting Kaizen activities into action and keeping track of their progress?

There are certain steps that top executives need to take in order to demonstrate their commitment to Kaizen.

Beginning of the Meeting: It is the moment that marks the official announcement to each employee of the company that the top executives have made regarding the official commencement of Kaizen operations. This demonstrates the top executives' deep commitment to Kaizen, which will result in an increase in employee motivation. Employees will see that their managers are attempting to expand the company's operations and productivity, which will make them feel more valued in their roles.

Identifying and Advocating for Deserving Kaizen Leaders: Help can be provided in the form of prompt selection and confirmation of kaizen leaders, authorization to carry out additional kaizen activities within the allotted work time, and other forms of tacit support that can be provided. Because of this, the entirety of the organization will be able to see how important Kaizen is.

On-site patrol: This includes going out onto the shop floors to gather information about the temperatures and conditions of the workplace, as well as maintaining the machinery. In order to keep their employees on their toes at all times, upper management needs to be aware of how everything is operating, and more importantly, they need to demonstrate that they are ready to check at any time.

A passion for attending Kaizen meetings: The level of dedication shown by top managers to Kaizen-related reforms will be made transparent by their participation in the process. It is important for the employees to observe all of this and become motivated as a result of it.

The level of investment required for Kaizen: One of the most important aspects of Kaizen is that it makes use of the resources already present within an organization rather than requiring the business to make significant new investments. Generally speaking, relatively little effort is required in terms of making large purchases and incurring additional costs in order to implement kaizen. Instead, it brings down the costs.

The diagnosis, as provided by top management: The highest-level managers are required to receive periodic updates from the QCC (Quality Control) team, after which they should evaluate the current state of the Kaizen activities. It is also a wonderful opportunity to communicate with the staff the perspectives of the top executives in the company. When it comes to bridging the gap between management and workers, this is a crucial juncture.

Any reward that is given to a person or a team is provided because they have generated amazing outcomes that helped in achieving the stability of Kaizen execution. This is the basis for the incentive system. This reward may take the form of cash, recognition from peers, an electronic gift card, or even cash itself. Everyone has their own unique idea of how they would like to be acknowledged; while some people would rather have a party in their honor, others would be satisfied with a simple email. It is essential to adapt the recognition system in accordance with the specific requirements of the employees at your company.

Before attempting to engage in training that is tailored specifically for Kaizen leaders, it is necessary to put in place an education system. This is done to ensure that the top executives are aware of the activities that were discussed earlier. This not only allows them to get a better grasp of Kaizen, but it also gives them the ability to share valuable knowledge and discuss problems with other companies' top managers. It can eventually lead to a collaborative environment where results and statistics can be shared to holistically develop better Kaizen techniques.

Leadership Development for the Kaizen Movement

The Functions of Kaizen Group Leaders

The Kaizen leaders are the ones who take the lead in all of the Kaizen activities, including enforcing the guidance that is given by both the Advanced Trainers and the Basic Trainers. Leadership and dedication are two of the most important factors that determine how successfully a Kaizen operation will function. The following responsibilities are obligatory for Kaizen leaders:

The Kaizen practices themselves should be carried out by Kaizen leaders, who should then report their progress to a Kaizen Trainer (s). Some of the things that they are capable of doing are the following:

Project QCC: A quality control circle is a group of employees who are overseen by a Kaizen leader and tasked with ensuring that Kaizen practices such as eliminating manufacturing errors, reducing waste, and implementing incremental change are carried out on a consistent basis.

Advice concerning the election of QCC's leadership

Helping QCC teams or individual members who are struggling to keep up with their activities

Another task that needs to be completed is the formulation of event plans, annual project plans, instructional plans, technological plans, financial plans, production of internal posters, preparation of badges and brochures, and other similar tasks. This is necessary in order to develop Kaizen activities and also to obtain prior approval from top managers for tasks related to Kaizen. They are also responsible for gathering progress reports and delivering them to the executives in charge of all Kaizen operations. In addition to this, they need to be involved in the process of planning presentations, delivering and checking data, and even taking leadership roles during conferences or meetings that are centered on Kaizen.

Instruction of Kaizen Group Leaders

The following are some of the activities that can be done to develop the capabilities and expertise of Kaizen leaders:

During the Kaizen training, participants shared their knowledge of the challenges they faced in open community discussions. Because the problems they are having are likely to be experienced by the staff of the entire organization, this will be of benefit to the entire organization. When these issues are dealt with as soon as they arise, it is easier to sort them out and understand the conundrums that arise.

Introducing practices that are related to Kaizen

mentoring and training sessions led by Intermediate Trainers, Basic Trainers, or Kaizen Experts.

Participating in and giving presentations on workshops and conferences pertaining to Kaizen.

The Management of Total Quality (TQM)

The term "kaizen" refers to the incorporation of various practices and programs, such as TQM and worker recommendations. What exactly does it mean to work with TQM? It is a movement that is centered on the goal of improving organizational efficiency at all levels of the company. The concepts of health, quality control, employee engagement, cost management, increased efficiency, and performance improvement are all included in Total Quality Management. People are essential to the accomplishment of the TQM cycle, and this aspect is given a lot of attention because the part of Kaizen in which they are involved is the one in which everyone participates. Under TQM, common practices include things like preparation, coordination, opportunity creation, and collective participation in the work that needs to be done.

The TQM process addresses issues relating to the organization's cross-functional leadership, as well as the expansion of the organization and an increase in the efficiency of the organization. TQM is both a resource and a philosophy that is used to improve the potential and accomplishments of individuals within the organization.

The Total Quality Management (TQM) methodology is a structured approach that is centered on the enhancement of an organization's quality. TQM integrates existing training programs, conventional management techniques, and cutting-edge methodological approaches. These efforts are, ultimately, geared toward ensuring an increase in the level of satisfaction experienced by customers. What needs to be emphasized is the fact that the innovative aspects of change can be mechanical, or they can be related to innovation. The relationship that individuals have with various forms of technology is the only factor that determines how susceptible they are to change. This indicates that changing people does nothing to foster innovation; the only thing that contributes to growth is changing how people work and how they relate to machines.

To achieve profitability, as well as to increase efficiency and quality, an organization needs to harness the potential that is lying dormant in the workforce. This can be accomplished by encouraging each employee to perform their work in the correct manner from the very beginning of their employment. This will also make it possible for upper-level managers to demonstrate to every employee in the company that every single one of them is required to demonstrate dedication to the success of the company as a whole and to make ongoing efforts to do so. As soon as the workers comprehend this, they will experience an increase in their level of motivation because they will understand the significance of their role in the achievement of the organization's goals.

It is imperative that the culture of the organization be one in which every worker voluntarily contributes to the accomplishment of the organization's goals. When workers are coerced into working, they often become disinterested in their work, which has a negative impact on productivity. This provides the management with the opportunity to consider any suggestions made by workers who are both willing to contribute to the success of the company and possess the ability to do so. The top management is simply communicating orders and priorities to the workers below them, and then they are leaving space for ideas to float upwards. This acts as a self-checking mechanism because, as orders move downward, they come into contact with workers who relay any potential problems with the order back upwards so that top management can address them and resolve them.

The TQM methodology is helpful because it provides specific ways in which a business can become more efficient. This is accomplished by conducting an investigation into the manner in which work is carried out from the perspective of orderliness, structure, consistency, and operation. The primary objectives of implementing the Total Quality Management method are to:

Meet the requirements of all domestic and international customers.

Involve every operational entity that the organization has, and make sure to leave no one out of the consideration zone.

A comprehension of the influence that heterogeneity has on the TQM processes, as well as the potential means of enhancing those processes.

To bring attention to the ongoing development of Kaizen.

Encouragement and participation on the part of workers should become the primary driving force behind improvements in the organization's productivity and profitability.

The TQM cycle will always result in dissatisfaction and disappointment if tolerance and patience are lacking throughout the process. The progression of the organization can not occur without having respect for one another and working well together. It is abundantly clear that employee engagement and process-oriented manufacturing strategies are significant factors and, as a consequence, the foundational pillars of total quality management (TQM). During the Kaizen session, the fundamental aspects for cultivating the individual members of the team and improving the capacity of the company to follow these processes are the structure and practices of the team.

The application of TQM to drive organizational enhancement is analogous to the Kaizen approach. Both of these things share characteristics and different parts, and it's possible that they only need one organizational structure to function properly. Combining the two approaches is the most effective strategy for achieving organizational success.

Three important factors are discussed: (QCD)

It is common knowledge that customers are the most important people in a market economy. As a result, the end goal of any company should be to satisfy the expectations of customers concerning the QCD of the products and services they provide. Improving QCD is the primary objective of Kaizen and all of its activities. Because of this, QCD should be one of the company's top priorities in order for it to thrive.

The quality of a product is what determines its value; this quality is developed, preserved, and preserved through a variety of processes, beginning with the procurement of raw materials and continuing through the phases of designing, developing, manufacturing, distributing, supplying, and even servicing the products or providing the services throughout the life cycle of the business. Imai mentioned that sketches and documentation are the first steps in the process of developing new products or services, as well as designing new engineered ones. Malfunctions can be quickly identified and fixed, whereas it would be very costly to fix them if they were discovered later on in the process. The Quality Function Deployment (QFD), also known as the Quality Assurance Process Diagram, was utilized by the management of Japanese companies as a tool in order to accomplish this objective.

After the quality of the product or service, the next most important factor to consider is how cost-effective it will be to create the product, manufacture it, market it to customers, and even provide the good or service that the company provides. It is more accurate to refer to this process as cost control rather than cost cutting. It is the responsibility of the management team that oversees expenses to monitor the production, marketing, and sale of low-priced goods or services of a high standard of quality. The manner in which a product is conceived, manufactured, and distributed will determine whether or not there will be an enormous loss of resources. The best option for continued existence is to simultaneously increase productivity while simultaneously lowering prices.

Management of costs involves a wide variety of practices, such as overall cost control, which involves reducing duplication and planning expenditures in order to increase the difference between revenue and expenditures. Only when the proper procedures for getting rid of waste, which were described earlier, are followed, will there be a decrease in the costs associated with doing so. The cycle of production will be disrupted if you try to cut costs by reorganizing, negotiating harshly with vendors, and laying off workers, and this will typically lead to a decline in product quality. Standardization, the implementation of regulations, training, and education are some of the other tasks that are included in effective administration for the purpose of lowering costs while simultaneously raising quality. At this time, the majority of companies are continuing to place an excessive amount of emphasis on instructing workers in various skills. Within the framework of Kaizen, a significant amount of focus is placed on further bolstering the organization's fundamental values, which are maintained by the community in an ongoing manner via learning and teaching programs.

Self-discipline, sound judgment, commitment to the group's culture, and a sense of fairness are the ideals that each member of the organization should strive to embody.

Chapter Three: Kaizen's Benefits

In this section, we are going to take a look at how kaizen helps businesses, people, and the entirety of our society. Kaizen can provide your organization with multiple benefits, and these are the benefits that we are going to discuss.

Motivation

People who do not fit into the fold of the organization can be shown respect, tamed, or fired, and workers can be inspired to take the same small steps that produce incremental change and find solutions to their problems. Respect, taming, and firing are all ways to generate motivation. As an illustration, the management is aware that the morale of the employees is quite low. They then hire people to fix this problem, which incurs additional costs and cuts into the companies' profits. In order to resolve this issue, they recruit people. They guarantee that they will improve employee happiness, which may include providing more breaks at work; however, this may end up having a negative impact on the productivity of the company. Instead, if the company had been able to maintain high levels of morale among its workforce, those workers would have continued to put in effort even when they were permitted to take a break, which would have resulted in significant cost savings for the business.

Increasing people's motivation to work hard is essential, and the only way this can happen is by paying them a fair wage for the work they've already done. People only want one thing, and that is to know that the work they put in at their jobs is appreciated. Small expressions of gratitude for the work that they have done are always appreciated by employees. There are many factors that can contribute to employee dissatisfaction, including recent layoffs, a freeze on pay increases, and the discontinuation of benefits previously provided to workers. The vast majority of employees appear to be aware that at any given time, the management of the company is not to blame for the company's financial woes; rather, these issues are a reflection of the economic climate. As was discussed earlier, the process of building long-term, sustainable success within the organization requires taking baby steps. Employee morale can be improved by providing opportunities for team building activities, such as "holding each other" tasks that can be completed in as little as five minutes per day. This does not mean that they have to physically support each other; rather, they should simply express gratitude for the contributions made by all members of the team so that no one has the impression that they are not a part of it.

After this has been taken care of, you will be able to go about your normal routine. It is not a reflection of their extroverted personalities or their abilities to orate when employees express gratitude to their managers for being excellent communicators. The explanation for this is that the leaders did what they were supposed to do and made the most of the limited opportunities that they have to communicate with their employees. They viewed their employees as intelligent people who were already doing a good job, so rather than barking orders at them, they talked to their employees.

You should make an effort to remember the names of the employees so that you can address your questions directly to them. Make sure you wait for people to answer your questions, and always show gratitude by saying "thank you." If you want to maintain a high level of morale in the workplace, you need to place an emphasis on the smaller interactions that take place there. One of the most significant problems that face corporations all over the world is low morale, but this issue can be remedied by showing appreciation to one's workforce for even a brief period of time each and every day.

You can put together a good team, but they won't be able to perform well if they aren't connected to each other early on in the process. Communicate with your employees right away. The requirement that we run a profitable enterprise is not the source of our motivation;

rather, our personal requirements are what drive us to succeed. Even the desire to turn a profit is tied to your aspirations, experiences, and feelings in some way. Therefore, the only way for your staff members to feel motivated is if they have a strong sense of connection to both you and the other members of the team.

You will have the opportunity to get to know people's personalities and needs, which will make it easier for you to motivate others in your role as the leader. You will be able to put them in the appropriate roles, modify your behavior to match theirs, and use their desires to motivate them into working harder if you go about it in this manner. You also do not need to be so covert about any of this; rather, by forming personal connections with your employees, you will be able to have more candid conversations with them. This will pave the way for a relationship in which you will be able to know what is affecting them, and you will be able to give them the appropriate advice to assist them in locating their motivation for work.

The top executives' attention is redirected by kaizen toward mundane but important tasks, such as having a one-on-one chat with each of their staff members, which they ordinarily neglect. As a result, employee motivation is increased. When the Kaizen philosophy is implemented throughout an entire organization, it will become second nature for individuals to express gratitude to one another for even the most insignificant of accomplishments. This is because individuals will begin to understand why it is important for even the most insignificant of accomplishments to be accomplished.

Savings on Expenses

Workers are required to get rid of any mechanism in the Kaizen cost management strategy that does not lead to an increase in the effectiveness and quality of the products and services they produce. In no way does the implementation of Kaizen in any organization compromise the health and safety of its workforce. Employees in Kaizen companies are expected to maintain a vigilant vigilance regarding the waste of vital resources. The company will remove a method from the list of permitted and encouraged activities if employees put it through its paces and find that it causes inconsistency in the products it manufactures or reduces their value. As a result, cost management becomes powerful and reliable.

It might just seem unproductive to rely on employees to control costs, but if they are asked to take small steps to save money for the company, then they will help manage costs for the company. This is particularly true if they are asked to take small steps to save money for the company.

Employees value being given a purpose, as doing so makes them feel more connected to the company, and it also encourages them to take the initiative.

It does not, however, give the management the right to put the responsibility for reducing costs on the shoulders of the employees and then leave them to their own devices to accomplish this task. To begin, this would instill a level of fear in the workforce, which would make it more difficult for any kind of advancement to be made. What needs to be done is to change the way in which employees think about the work they do on a day-to-day basis for the company so that they are better able to identify areas in which costs can be cut. They are going to become your most valuable asset once you allow them the autonomy to think for themselves and begin placing importance on the contributions they make.

As the manager, it is your responsibility to assist them in overcoming their fear of being judged by you as well as their fear of making suggestions that are illogical or ridiculous. Give your employees room to think creatively and show appreciation for their out-of-the-box suggestions.

The employee recommendation programs in Japan appear to be reliably effective, whereas the situation is quite the opposite in the United States. An investigation found that employers in the United States of America offer monetary bonuses to their workers that are proportional to the amount of money that the company was able to save as a direct result of the employee's recommendation. The fact that the workers will be able to keep any savings they make serves as an incentive for them to look for other ways to cut costs.

In contrast to Japan, the financial incentives offered here are either very meager or nonexistent altogether. Experiments in psychology have demonstrated how multifaceted and intricate human motivation can be. Motivation can come from either the outside or from within an individual. Our psychological requirements are the source of the inborn creativity that we all possess. In addition to taking pride in our work, we would like to contribute to the success of collaborative endeavors, be involved in positive projects, and work as part of a team. People want to be challenged with goals that they can accomplish and feel proud of what they have accomplished. They are driven by an innate urge to create things that are significant and have an influence that extends beyond themselves. The satisfaction of an extrinsic need requires something external to the individual. Some of the external characteristics, such as wealth and fame, can act as motivators. People are encouraged to continue working in stressful jobs by the external motivations that they face. The key to successfully cutting costs is to provide as few incentives as possible to employees. When an individual's deepest desires are satisfied, they experience a greater sense of motivation; however, when money is all that is offered to them, they become less concerned. This is the reason why providing monetary bonuses as a form of reward has the opposite effect intended.

While many managers want to make sure that their employees deliver quality work, some of them are so set in their ways that it actually works against them and causes them to fall behind. Managers who are authoritarian and push the limits of their employees usually end up causing more harm. The use of such methods will not result in the things being completed as easily and effectively as you would like them to be; rather, the employee will feel humiliated and uncomfortable working in your presence as a result of your actions. They will be so terrified of you that the answers they provide to your questions will be ambiguous, and they will never answer them with conviction. A question such as "how can the company make millions in profits while saving thousands of dollars?" is a good example of one that leaves all employees speechless. Even the most astute manager will be incapable of providing a response to a question of this nature, and the workers will be mute throughout the entire exchange. What you need to do is use a gentler approach by asking, "Do you think the company can save a bit of money here and there?" in order to achieve the desired results. You should encourage the employee to think about topics that, in their opinion, should not be considered while they are working. You have limitless opportunities to institutionalize change with Kaizen, and one of those opportunities is simply encouraging employees to think for themselves.

In addition to this, you could hang up notice boards in which individuals can post their ideas. Be sure that those suggestion boards are emptied every day and that you read through all of the comments because doing so will reassure employees that their feedback is being considered.

The employees are wary of making suggestions because they don't want to risk getting on your bad side. They keep any idea they have for cutting costs in the back of their minds, but only if their feedback is strongly focused on and they are encouraged to speak up about it. When Kaizen has been successfully implemented, workers will be tasked with identifying potential areas in which costs can be reduced. This does not imply that you do not have control as a manager or that you will not be given permission to take any action. You are in charge of analyzing the usefulness of the previous suggestions, which entails reviewing the ideas that have already been provided. You need to establish processes for the management of suggestions in order to standardize the performance of this duty. When going through the list of recommendations that was given to you, make sure you give every suggestion due consideration.

Keep in mind that there will be times when the suggestions will seem ridiculous, but if you look past that, you might find a fantastic idea. Sometimes the most immature ideas are the ones that hold the key to creativity. Do not forget to express your gratitude to the employees whose suggestions were responsible for the desired improvement at the company.

Chapter Eight

Greater Responsibility and Obligation

You should make it a goal to improve your ability to identify simple mistakes. These types of errors may at first appear to be very annoying and trivial, but if they are not addressed as soon as possible, they may develop into quality control issues later on. In kaizen, we are challenged to identify and rectify errors while they are still in their earliest stages. It might be tempting to ignore these problems before they become catastrophes, but that would be a mistake. When an organization consistently presents itself in an impressive manner, many businesses are willing to overlook relatively minor errors.

If a business is successful, it will ensure that the people who contributed to that success as well as the administrative processes will continue to receive honor and respect. It is impossible to bring to light any aspect of a company's operations that are not functioning as they should. The majority of people, on the other hand, choose to ignore the mistakes, and as a result, they miss out on the opportunity to improve themselves and better compete with others. Mark their assurance as a red flag any time you ask your employees if there are any issues that need to be addressed and they respond that there are none. The idea that individuals are going to act erratically at times is an essential presumption of the Kaizen methodology.

Keep in mind that every person is ultimately responsible for the organization as a whole. In light of this, you should not shy away from accountability, and you should teach your employees to do the same. Develop the ability to spot these insignificant blunders, make it clear that you expect everyone else in the company to notice them as well, and offer them the solutions they need to address these problems. According to the tenets of kaizen, everyone in an organization, regardless of the level on which they work, is responsible for the organization's effectiveness and profitability. The management of the organization also needs to make it simple for workers on lower levels to communicate their feedback and suggestions with executives on higher levels.

Innovation

There is a widespread misconception that the modest improvements we make in accordance with the Kaizen methodology will only yield insignificant outcomes. In point of fact, these seemingly insignificant actions that we carry out eventually result in significant innovations that alter the world over a period of time. When we start paying attention to those little moments in life that might otherwise seem insignificant, we start to become more creative, which is the precursor to innovation. Questions are the starting point for creative thinking in the business world because they allow us to bridge the gap between reality and imagination. By asking what is missing and what might be wrong, we can discover what is not there. Imagination is the driving force behind productive programs, the creation of new products, and improvements. In spite of the fact that innovative thinking can be utilized at any time, there are specific circumstances in which it has the potential to shine brightest and have the most significant effect. These moments occur when actual work is being done; the only time we can find the radical potential that imagination gives us to make our work better is when we have completely invested ourselves in our work. These moments occur when actual work is being done. There are also the following instances of innovation:

Loss of efficiency: If something is out of alignment, time is wasted; if something ends up breaking, composure is lost; as a result, we will either have to reorganize our schedule or fix the object that has been broken. When situations like this arise, you should approach them with an inquisitive attitude because wherever there is wastefulness, there is also the possibility for change.

Shame: Quite frequently, it is shame that stimulates one's curiosity due to the fact that there is a gap between what has been done and what should have been done. It goes without saying that this is an uncomfortable sensation, and it is natural to try to avoid feeling it by, for example, trying to keep the error a secret from people who have not yet been informed about it. There are a lot of people who will admit that they have done something wrong, and some of them will even laugh at the fact that they did it, all in an effort to move on with their lives as quickly as they can. In that context, ingenuity might consist of making an attempt to conceal the error in some way.

When all is said and done, what you'll realize is that imagination does not call for any special kind of talent. It simply requires us to concentrate on the activity that we are currently engaged in. You need to practice self-discipline if you want to maintain a state of constant concentration and curiosity. The steps of Kaizen will not only help you maintain your attentiveness but will also provide the excitement you require. If you want to strengthen your imagination, you can use another technique from the Kaizen methodology, which is to pay attention to the mistakes that have been made. It is a paradox that mistakes must be made in order for creativity to be triggered, but at the same time, nobody wants to make mistakes. Creativity can only be triggered by a trial and error approach. As a result, the most effective strategy for resolving this conundrum is to develop modest pilot projects and to actively encourage errors that serve as opportunities for education while simultaneously bringing down overall expenses. When you begin to reap the benefits of innovation, you will reflect back on the tenacity that was required to bring such creativity into existence. Therefore, patience is a valuable resource that can result in benefits over the longer term.

Better Sales

No matter how hard you try to comprehend it, the sales industry is always terrifying. Sales are an act of manipulation that encourages other people to trade money for products and services, with the overt goal of paying the money being support for the company's ideas. Sales are also an activity that encourages the exchange of money for products and services. The job of a salesman is to sell the products and services that they are required to sell in exchange for compensation, while also selling themselves and their company. However, the world typically has the impression that they are not generous people. The salesman is required to keep pushing until their job is finished, which means that whatever it is that they are required to sell has been sold, despite the fact that many people respond to them with hostility and dismissal.

There are a lot of people who are nervous about making sales calls, and Kaizen was created specifically for those individuals. The majority of salespeople despise the feeling of anxiety that arises whenever they consider the required level of product turnover that they must accomplish. Kaizen is an excellent resource for both recruiting new sales workers and retraining existing ones. The use of kaizen is highly recommended, particularly in tense circumstances. A significant portion of us have been socialized to mentally retreat whenever we are confronted with challenging conditions. That in and of itself does not make anyone a poor salesperson. It is merely a physiological reaction that the individual has no control over. When confronted with challenges that appear to be insurmountable, the amygdala in the brain registers a sense of impending danger to our very existence.

It is better than you should choose those as salesmen whose brains instinctively appreciate the excitement that comes with sales, but such people tend to burn out quickly and easily. For a salesperson, the cost of training can be quite high, and dropping out of the program is both unreliable and expensive. The question that needs to be asked is why the majority of management companies do not teach their sales departments how to use Kaizen techniques to deal with anxiety and stress. Getting past one's anxiety to the point where one can think clearly and concentrate on one step at a time is the goal of the fear management technique, which is based on the Kaizen method. Empowering the workers to make subtle shifts in the way they approach problems is preferable to mandating behavioral changes among the workforce.

Keeping your mind at ease and motivating you to keep moving forward will require you to take baby steps toward the larger goal. It's not uncommon for a course of action to appear intimidating or frightening, or for you to experience emotional strain if it seems like it will be difficult to carry out such significant steps. In a situation like this, what options do you have? The shaping of one's mental image comes into play at this point. Mind-sculpting is just one of the many fundamental tools used in Kaizen. It's a technique for getting rid of the emotional resistance that all of us have. Directed imagery was the foundation on which the practice of mind sculpting was built. The objective was to guide patients through the process of mastering a particular physical ability without actually having them perform the skill. If a patient's goal is to increase their ability to vocalize, for instance, the patient will close their eyes and take several deep breaths. After the individual had reached a state of ease, the psychologist prompted them to imagine themselves inside a dimly lit movie theater, where they were very quietly seated in front of an empty screen. At that point, it is normal for the patient to hear a voice presenting a demonstration that is shown on the screen.

The practice of mind sculpture seeks to build upon the knowledge that other psychologists have gained from the method of guided imaging. It is a sensory experience that is only imagined, but it is experienced in its entirety. You don't have to pretend to be in a movie theater if you don't want to; you can imagine yourself performing any

activity instead. Imagine yourself in the role
of a salesperson and play out the sales call
in your head over and over again. When
injuries prevented them from engaging in
traditional forms of training, athletes turned
to a sculpting mentality to get their workouts
in. When they get back out there, they are
more successful than they have ever been
before. Mind modeling is also used in the music
industry. It is nothing more than a method
of training the brain by visualizing different
scenarios and teaching it to react appropriately
to each one.

Put yourself in your mind's eye in a stressful
sales situation, for instance, if you seem to
respond to your anxiety by either speaking too
quickly or emotionally withdrawing yourself
from the situation. Imagine dealing with the
predicament in a way that you won't be able
to in actuality because it's impossible. Imagine

that every part of your body is releasing its stress at the same time. Now, in this situation, you should start to gradually bring the other person into reality. Imagine the possibilities that would arise if you asked the right questions, met the customers' expectations, and actively sought to understand their requirements. You need to gradually improve your self-assurance and the clarity of your voice.

You should try to give yourself at least thirty seconds per day to work on your mental sculpting. Make an effort to extend the amount of time you put into practice once you notice that the activities you complete each day are becoming less taxing on you and even more routine. The degree to which you take pleasure in performing the exercise of mind sculpting will determine how quickly you advance in your ability to do so. You should not increase the time until the entire exercise is able to be completed without much effort.

The amount of time spent on continuous mind sculpting should be increased until one of two potential outcomes has been achieved. The first thing to do is lay the groundwork for the future improvements. During the course of the practice, you need to focus on achieving a state of relaxation. You need to have the mindset that you are prepared to carry out the activity, even if your go-to strategy is to tackle it one baby step at a time. You might also need someone to practice sales with, preferably a friend who is someone you are already familiar with. You can pick someone who scares you if you want to give yourself a challenge, or you can pick someone who is more experienced than you are. The second possibility is that with little or no additional deliberate effort on your part, your brain will automatically become good at the task, and it may even create new patterns that you may not have even practiced. This occurs whether or not you are aware of this happening. You could be in the middle of a sales call when unexpected new ideas for lines would start running through your head.

When you are in a challenging sales situation and see yourself using words as easily as you have been practicing, you will know that mind sculpting has worked perfectly for you. You will know this when it has happened. You will know that you have reached a level of mastery in sales when things that previously caused you to feel awkward and forget what you were going to say now come to you instinctively, and when things that previously seemed impossible to achieve become commonplace for you.

Mind sculpting is a technique that can be very useful for instilling new behaviors in people with as little as a few minutes of practice per day, or even less. The brain learns new skills through the process of repetition, which is then stored in the neural pathways and cells. As a result of this, advertisements are constantly pushed throughout the day because the advertiser is aware that this is the only way to effectively communicate with your brain.

Beneficial Employees

In those days, nobody would have dreamed that executives would feel responsible for the well-being of their employees. However, they do so now because the cost of providing health insurance to employees has ballooned to an enormous level for businesses. It is now required of businesses to provide their employees with health insurance coverage. This is to the advantage of businesses because if an employee continues to call out sick and miss work, it will eventually result in the company losing a significant amount of money. When an employee's health is stable, not only is the amount of labor they produce consistent, but also the rate at which they produce it. This results in cost savings for the company. Marathons and other endurance competitions are becoming increasingly commonplace as a result of the growing concern that businesses have for the well-being of their workforce. The company is now not only concerned with your ability to come to work, but also cares about what you're doing outside of it, what you're eating, and whether or not you are taking good care of yourself or not. The majority of businesses are finally coming to the realization that their employees are resources, and that it is difficult to find replacements for skilled employees. When an employee gets sick, it is more expensive for a company to hire a replacement worker than it is to invest in the health of an employee who is already productive.

Many businesses realize the importance of keeping their employees in good health and therefore provide incentives for employees who achieve a desired weight loss. They incentivize their workers by encouraging competition between departments, and whichever department loses the most weight as a whole wins a day off for all of its employees. It is possible that such rewards will be successful in the short term; however, in the long run, they will be unsuccessful due to the fact that once the program is over, the employees will return to their previous habits. What supervisors need to realize is that getting rid of excess weight is the single most difficult goal a person can have because it necessitates a fundamental shift in the way of life they have cultivated for themselves over the years. This includes altering how they think, caring more about their health, and having enough motivation to perform better. Why is it so difficult to exercise this level of self-control? What are the obstacles that stand in the way?

The most significant factor in this is apprehension. The idea behind kaizen is that people are resistant to change in general due to the fact that they are ingrained in their routines and enjoy having a sense of order in their lives. They end up feeling anxious because there are too many changes. The fear factor that is associated with making significant changes to one's lifestyle is alleviated through the use of the Kaizen method, which is effective in these kinds of circumstances. People have a tendency to think more clearly and become capable of appreciating the benefits of a healthier lifestyle once their fears have been alleviated.

But how exactly do you show your staff that Kaizen is an effective method for addressing their various health concerns? You only need to convey to them the significance of incorporating kaizen into their day-to-day lives and that's it! By subdividing each and every job into more manageable chunks, you will find that virtually everything starts to become simpler. Once you accept Kaizen as a way of life, you will begin to see the world in a different light; this is because Kaizen is a philosophy, and not just a business strategy. Because of this, once Kaizen has been incorporated into the workforce, it completely creates a great many added benefits that you might not have even thought of. Because people will start living healthier lives, which will result in fewer health issues, the amount of money you spend on maintaining the health of your workforce will decrease, which will lead to a reduction in the amount of money you spend on maintaining the health of your workforce. The kaizen philosophy is an all-encompassing one, and its influence can be felt both inside and outside of the organization.

Chapter Nine

Kaizen and Startups

Now that you understand what the theory is all about, you have a lot of options to implement Kaizen in your new startup business so that you can achieve a strategic advantage right from the beginning. Every person who starts a new business with the goal of selling a lot of their product or service has this dream. There are some people who will never see their dreams come true. It is estimated that only one entrepreneur out of every three thousand will be able to pave their way to victory and development, which will allow their startup to skyrocket. This is not a matter of blind fate or random chance at all. It is the result of making well-considered judgments and cultivating an environment that is always changing and expanding! Things will only occur if there is an environment that is conducive to both learning and development.

To gain an advantage over competing businesses, newly established businesses should make sure their employees are well-versed in how to handle potential changes, obstacles, and innovations. The most important thing is to educate the current workforce so that they, in turn, can educate any potential workers who might join the workforce in the future. A learning culture is one that brings about change, ongoing progress, and enhancement for any and every business.

This is the key to successfully creating an environment in which feedback, ideas, and innovations can be freely discussed. When everyone is included in the decision-making process, every worker at the company will experience the feeling of being a stakeholder in the business. If you want your business to develop into an institutional power that can compete with other businesses, you should provide your employees with training that teaches them not only to obey orders but, more importantly, how to make decisions.

Applying Kaizen

If you want to apply Kaizen to your startup, the following is a list of the areas and principles on which you should concentrate your efforts:

Constructing a Group

As was mentioned in the preceding chapter, the core of the Japanese Kaizen theory revolves around the formation of powerful teams. In keeping with the tenets of the Kaizen tradition, the group will be comprised of knowledgeable workers who are also prepared to challenge established hierarchies. It is necessary for there to be a shift in the status quo in order to make meaningful and systemic changes the focus of your efforts. Maintaining a consistent status quo is antithetical to the tenets of the Kaizen philosophy. Transformation and continuous progress toward a goal are absolutely necessary for the successful application of the Kaizen theory.

Enhancement

What are some different ways that quality improvement can be developed in a startup? You need to start concentrating on things like brainstorming, coming up with ideas, creating an open-door policy for feedback, developing a less hierarchical organizational structure, and other similar activities. This is where the process of data collection comes into play. Gathering information about your company should begin on the very first day. Make use of this knowledge to determine what is working for the company and what is not working for it. When it comes to new businesses, it's usually a bad idea to get rid of failing systems right away because it's possible that you won't have all of the relevant information just yet because the system hasn't been operational for very long. The accumulation of information over a period of time will assist you in making decisions that are relatively reliable and in abandoning unsuccessful systems over the course of time. You might not have access to nearly as many records as a businessman or company founder does. On the other hand, they are essential for making decisions over the long term as well as terminating programs that have not been successful. Collect the necessary information, make an analysis of it, and figure out what changes need to be made in order for the business to have a successful future.

Chapter Ten

Putting Changes Into Effect

The inability of a company to reconfigure its processes, strategies, and structures in order to adapt to modern, more cost-effective, and more successful ways of doing things is the most significant obstacle to development. Consider how these shifts will influence the expansion of the company. To get started, you should determine how the changes will affect things over the course of one month. In order to guarantee that the adjustments are effective, the next step is to conduct an analysis of the effects that any administrative, procedural, or other kinds of improvements have had over the course of a year. It will also assist you in visualizing what the company will look like in the future and will serve as an essential guiding pillar.

Contextualizing Kaizen to Startup Culture

Because kaizen is fundamentally based on teamwork, it is imperative that each and every member of your workforce be involved in the development of its policies and procedures. They ought to be given the opportunity to communicate their ideas, logical deductions, insights, and feedback on business matters as if they were their very own. To improve business operations, increase employee productivity, reduce costs, and enhance quality and safety standards are some of the goals that will be addressed in the ideas and recommendations that will be presented.

The workers need to be motivated in order
for them to actively participate in their own
ideas and thoughts as well as understand
what those activities entail. The resources
necessary to recruit a specialist in Kaizen
are beyond those of a startup. You can
solve this problem by recognizing the more
nuanced aspects of the Japanese revolutionary
ideology of kaizen and beginning to use
it to achieve your managerial and business
goals through the process of holding kaizen
workshops. The staff members will receive
motivation to achieve a rating in the six
sigma business practices. There are also other
training methods that you should encourage,
such as project management, which can help
increase their overall performance by reducing
errors and optimizing the working structure of
the manufacturing process. If you encourage

these methods, you can help increase their overall performance.

Advice and Instructions

The participation of workers in the process of change and improvement is only one aspect of kaizen. The following is a list of some of the theory of Kaizen's most helpful hints and tips, which will instruct you on what to do and what to avoid when it comes to applying it in your company:

Do not put all of your eggs in one basket by relying solely on your previous experiences, and do not place an irrational amount of stock in your own abilities in comparison to those of others. If you want to develop a business that is both profitable and innovative, you should look to other people on the team for their talents, insights, knowledge, and expertise. By adhering to rigid structures and procedures, your performance will suffer, which will give your competitors an advantage in the game.

Do not wait around for the perfect moment to come along. You can reimagine a company even if there is only a forty percent chance of success, and you can continue to grow and make advancements along the way. You will only end up in a state of stagnation if you wait until everything is in its proper location before taking action.

Do not lose sight of the problems and difficulties. Fix them as soon as you become aware of them, rather than ignoring them or waiting for the perfect moment to do so. Learning is easiest to do while doing something else. The longer you choose to disregard the insignificant issues that your startup faces on a daily basis, the more severe those issues will become, and the more they will hinder the company's overall profitability, performance, and advancement.

Do not be hesitant when it comes to telling other people about something you don't understand and asking for some assistance with it. Just because something isn't clear to you doesn't mean you should make it more difficult for other people to understand what's going on. It is especially important to have discussions and debates at the beginning of the process rather than allowing confusion to take root and an incomplete understanding of the processes, procedures, and technologies to develop over the course of the project.

The practice of basing decisions solely on opinions rather than facts and figures is one of the most common and significant mistakes made by new businesses. Because it's a brand-new endeavor, everyone is eager to share their opinion on the matter. However, in terms of both productivity and performance, this tactic is not very effective. To the fullest extent possible, consider all recommendations and suggestions. However, you should make sure that they are supported by the facts whenever it is possible to obtain them. It is important to keep in mind that decisions are not made in the conference room while sipping on cups of coffee. This indicates that the majority of decision making consists of only thirty percent debate and seventy percent decisions that are made instinctively while performing daily functional activities.

Maintain the mindset that you do not have it in good order, and that you need to make changes to everything. You need to make the pursuit of quality growth, transformation, and enhancement your goal. This is especially true in the case of a startup, which is in the process of continuously testing a variety of structures, both organizational and operational, to evaluate and determine what functions most effectively for the entire company.

Guide to Instilling Kaizen Changes

Determine which aspects of your business are necessary before continuing on with your Kaizen journey.

Even though, traditionally speaking, Kaizen methods are connected to the production and manufacturing industry, just like Six Sigma, it is now being used in all different kinds of trade and other different industries. Establish routines that can be applied to your startup on a daily, weekly, and monthly basis. You will be able to concentrate more on improving the procedures as a result. It is essential to have some cash reserves ready at all times in order to manage and organize the cash flow. Prepare for unexpected emergencies involving a lack of cash by having a company credit card and other credit lines available. The best time to put in place documents that can easily guide all aspects of the company is when the procedures are not already in place (which is the case with a lot of startups). Do not put all of your knowledge and trust in the abilities of just one person. One of the most significant blunders that new businesses regularly make is placing an excessive amount of weight on the experience and expertise of the company's founders rather than establishing adequate documentation. This implies that whenever a problem arises, the employees are required to seek the expertise of the company's founder rather than looking up what steps to take next in a structured procedural guide. The Kaizen process should not be carried out in such an unhealthy manner. A fruitful application of the Kaizen methodology requires not only the recording of all consistency processes but also the provision of opportunities for all members of the team to review processes whenever they see fit. You will be able to construct better products and more efficient processes if you proceed in this manner. There may be some outmoded processes that can be eliminated, modified, or reworked, which will result in significant cost reductions.

Which aspects of the business are absolutely essential to the operation of the organization, as they are the ones that propel or drive the company forward? Carry out our routine training and assessments, and use the data to inform your efforts at continuous improvement. When procedures are recorded, it is much simpler to find ways to improve them by recognizing areas in which they are lacking.

Your company will eventually experience growth, at which point the competitive landscape will have shifted significantly. You will need to adjust to the new policies and procedures that have been implemented as well as adapt to the new developments. This is going to be extremely important to the success of your startup.

Take into consideration the following elements in order to successfully implement Kaizen into your startup: What is it exactly that you are doing right now? In what ways could things be improved? Is it even remotely possible for you to adjust what it is that you are doing right now, even if the adjustment is only slight? It is possible that you should modify the way in which you handle your invoices so that, rather than spending a few hours each day managing them, you handle them all collectively on a Saturday or Sunday in order to simplify the process of paying invoices. You can improve the performance of your company by applying the Kaizen theory, and there are a lot of questions like this that you can ask yourself that will show you the way to go about doing so successfully.

Inspire the Workforce to Carry Out Constant Adaptations.

Is the work environment at the company positive and inviting for employees who want to offer creative suggestions or constructive feedback? If this is not the case, then your company will require a Kaizen solution in order to move forward. When running a startup, it is even more important to keep employees motivated and to solicit original ideas and suggestions from them. It would make them feel more a part of the start-up and boost overall engagement, both of which will lead to more ethical behavior on the part of your employees. Consider the following: when an employee is given the opportunity to make a suggestion within your recently established business, and that employee's recommendation is implemented, the employee feels valuable, respected, and motivated, which leads to the employee coming up with even more ideas for change and development within the company. Give the workers the autonomy to decide how to deal with any problems that they discover. In an ideal scenario, the operation of the company and the making of decisions will be overseen by a manager or another similarly competent individual. They should, as a result, have the creative control necessary to solve problems and develop processes that will make their tasks more effectively. Once those procedures have been figured out, they will be communicated to the rest of the team.

Nevertheless, it is essential for workers to have the belief that they have the ability to make things better in any situation in which they are experiencing issues. Inspire and encourage the staff to think of innovative, resourceful, and creative ways to improve their work processes and their assignments. Motivate them to look for opportunities to change the way they do things, and encourage them to share their discoveries with others. Begin by celebrating even the smallest victories to lay the groundwork for a community that is dedicated to continuous improvement. Every employee at your company ought to have the impression that they are actively encouraged to participate in the decision-making process or to make their own decisions. It is essential for small businesses because you are at an early stage in the process where the role of each employee is essential. They are all early members of the team or founding members, which gives them the impression that they play an important role in the development, culture, and history of the organization. When you encourage these already essential employees to make decisions, you can help them feel even more deeply about their position in the company. [Case in point:] It is not unheard of for a single person to embody the entire organization in a small company or startup. Because of this, it is essential to have clear lines of communication.

When an employee communicates with you, you should listen carefully, take their comments, and reviews into consideration. They have the ability to provide you with ground-level perspectives on something that your eye has probably overlooked. They are the ones who actually get their hands dirty working on a variety of procedures and programs, and as a result, they learn more effectively. I would encourage them to investigate what works well and what does not work well. Realize that they are experts in the processes that are unique to their company, and that they should carefully examine how those processes work. Because of this very reason, you can put your faith in them, and you should go after them to gain their knowledge.

When you begin to implement the Kaizen philosophy within your organization, you will come to the realization that no piece of information, regardless of its magnitude, is unimportant. Everything is important and contributes to the bigger picture. Any chance to show even the tiniest inkling of progress should be appreciated, even if it's just a little bit. Modifications of a minor nature will result in the accumulation of points, which, over the course of some period of time, will gradually accumulate into significant enhancements. This applies to everything to do with the company, not just its outgoing financial obligations. There are a variety of different ways in which waste can be discovered; anything that takes up the time of an employee or even the actual or virtual storage space ought to be investigated and checked as a potential field for the implementation of Kaizen.

Be aware of the fact that advancement or improvement are not the destination of this journey. This is not the end goal; rather, it is a belief that one must continue to follow the discovery and the subsequent progress that arises from the discovery. Kaizen is not about arriving at a destination; rather, it is about constantly moving forward and never letting up on the pursuit of improvement. It strives for steady improvement, one baby step at a time. Techniques for continuous learning and development need to be closely associated with the structure of the company and should also be a fundamental component of the culture of the organization. You shouldn't restrict the application of Kaizen to particular processes or to a few particular occasions only. It ought to be ingrained as a way of life into the corporate culture of the organization as a whole.

Developing a Mentality for Victory and Success

Working for a company with a "no" culture in the past can leave you feeling unmotivated because you are forced to perform in an atmosphere in which you are told something is impossible, despite the fact that you are aware that it is possible. In the past, you may have attempted to use a cutting-edge

program, method, or technology, only to be
informed that you are not permitted to do
so. Would you really want to cultivate such a
poisonous atmosphere within your brand-new
company? Eliminate a "no" mentality within
your organization if you want it to thrive and
be successful over the long term. Teach your
employees to always assume that something
is possible, even if they don't know for sure,
and to always answer "yes." With the right
frame of mind, one can accomplish anything,
from being open to novel concepts to assisting
a business in its long-term expansion and
success. Culture that says "yes" is founded
on the idea of fostering growth, modifying
existing systems, and assisting others in
moving forward together.

Pareto Principle

If you want to see a significant improvement in your performance, you should begin applying the Pareto Principle, also known as the 80/20 rule. The primary component of this strategy is breaking a large task down into a series of smaller ones in order to maximize its chances of success. The owners of small businesses and start-ups should encourage their employees to look for "big wins" for the company. These are situations in which the company can make the fewest efforts possible while still gaining the most benefit. That does not mean, however, that you should ignore the nuances that are present. Please keep in mind that this information will either make or break your business. Those who work in the service industry, those who design software, those who manufacture goods, and others could all stand to gain significantly from paying closer attention to the tiniest of details and making any necessary adjustments. For instance, a modest enhancement to the manufacturing process can convert a five percent decrease in material waste into a five percent decrease in the cost of the inputs required for production. Over a period of time, this 5% of the total will accumulate to become a significant sum.

Continual Metamorphosis

Alterations are only made at predetermined points in time throughout the year at other businesses. It is not recommended that your business start a practice like this one, in which improvements and updates are only accepted during certain times of the year. You should not restrict upgrades to a select few times throughout the year or to general meetings only. Regularly and continuously, without interruption, the process should be updated and the program improved. Make it something that is done routinely as part of the organization's culture. Create an enterprise that is driven by change from the very beginning of your startup's existence.

If your employees are aware that each day brings the possibility of learning something new, they will look forward to coming to work. They will be motivated to continue making improvements within the company as a result of the development goals, principles, and ideology that have been established. When workers realize there is a more efficient way to complete a task and realize they are free to implement this improved method, they will look forward to coming to work each day because they will know they are contributing to the company's success. They should be given the freedom to make decisions based on what they believe is best for the overall quality control, growth, efficiency, and competitiveness of the company, and they should be permitted to celebrate even the smallest of victories.

Even employees who aren't particularly creative can occasionally surprise their bosses with insightful suggestions that can boost the overall revenue of their companies and cut costs. When this occurs, it creates a true win-win circumstance for each and every company, which is precisely what Kaizen is all about. The concept of Kaizen emphasizes making relatively uncomplicated improvements. This fundamental but cutting-edge Japanese theory does not have a silver bullet that will solve the problems or make the obstacles vanish with a single pull of the trigger. Because Kaizen translates to "change for the better," its straightforward nature makes it stand out from other concepts. This is because, despite the fact that it may only involve a slight enhancement, the focus of Kaizen is on achieving ongoing progress. Change one aspect of the system at a time, and eventually the entire thing will be different.

Everyone enjoys listening to accounts of dramatic upheavals that bring about instantaneous improvements. The implementation of a number of incremental and methodical changes at both the individual and organizational levels is, on the other hand, a solution that is both more feasible and more effective.

The way that it operates on a psychological level is that significant shifts trigger the mechanism of fear and resistance from within our brain, which in turn shuts off our capacity to think logically and creatively. On the other hand, actions that are more manageable and streamlined prevent us from feeling tense, anxious, or scared. It does not set off the alarms or trigger the reflexive defense mechanisms that are present in our brain. When there is a gradual and steady change occurring in a way that is both long-lasting and efficient, our imaginative, rational, and cognitive processes work much more smoothly. Because of this, many people continue to believe that the strategy of being methodical and consistent is effective.

In a similar vein, doing the same thing over and over again makes it much easier for behaviors to be transformed into habits, which, in turn, become our way of life. The mind experiences a profound sense of contentment when it is able to accomplish even the smallest of tasks. Instead of making radical changes that might make you uncomfortable, continue to make gradual and incremental improvements to processes and systems on a consistent basis. Your emotional blindfolds are overcome when you make changes that are small and incremental, as opposed to making changes that are large and drastic, which cause work-related stress to take over and prevent you from accepting change with all of your heart. Even people who believe they are immune to fear will experience anxiety as a result of the change.

Chapter Eleven

The Ikigai Chapter

The term 'ikigai' is derived from the Japanese words 'iki,' which means 'life,' and 'kai,' which can be translated as either 'product' or 'value.' Ikigai is based on the idea that there is either something that exists outside of your own life or something that could eventually become a part of your own life, and that this something gives meaning to everything that is going on around you, including yourself, the people you live with, the place you live, and the environment. That is your Ikigai, the reason you were put on this earth. When you live your life with a purpose in mind, you always have a clear idea of what you should be doing, where you should be, and how you should be conducting yourself. The key is to get rid of those nagging questions that cause you to question everything in your environment.

Finding your ikigai enables you to live a much simpler and more purposeful life because you now have a clearer understanding of why you are here. During the good times, it will give you something that you want more than anything else, something that will help you get through the tough times, and something that will create a sense of accomplishment at the end of the day, allowing you to sleep comfortably in your bed at night. You won't have to waste time trying to find answers to pointless questions about existence as you get started on your day.

In today's world, it is common for many people to stumble upon their ikigai by accident. They wind up starting a family, getting their dream job, going on their first trip, penning a book, gaining self-assurance, or coming up with a new invention, and all of a sudden, they realize that this is exactly what it was that they had always wanted to do. They have come to the realization that this was the purpose of their life, and now they want nothing more than to live and die for this purpose. This is their contribution to the cosmos, their commitment to the entirety of the world, and their raison d'être in this life.

Some people in today's society are exposed to this information at an early age; a good number of educators and medical professionals are aware of this. Even when they were too young to comprehend how they could enter such professions, they were drawn to the idea of educating others or caring for others in some capacity. In their eyes, it is not merely work; rather, it is a calling that speaks to a higher purpose. This kind of motivation comes from within, and it comes from knowing that you have the potential to achieve great things, such as becoming an artist. There is also a possibility that this will occur at random at times.

For some, this realization arrives after years of searching their soul; however, for the majority of people, even after years of aimless wandering, nothing significant occurs. The vast majority of people, if they even bother to look for it, do not find their personal ikigai until they are in their forties or later in life. It is also possible for it to lead to mistakes, such as when you end up opening a business to which you didn't feel a genuine connection, which can leave you with a profound sense of regret. Many more people go through life without ever locating their personal ikigai or understanding the significance of their existence. They ultimately experience feelings of depression as a result of realizing that their efforts were fruitless. This sense of disconnection from your higher purpose causes you to have the impression that life is not something that should be lived.

To better appreciate the significance of Ikigai, let's look at Okinawa as a case study. Okinawa is a small island located to the south-west of Japan, but it has a population that is surprisingly large and robust. The notorious "Blue Zone" encompasses Okinawa as a whole. People in this region have a life expectancy that is significantly higher than that of traditional Westerners. Okinawans are known for their strong sense of inner motivation and intention, in addition to their tight-knit community. Ikigai is the driving force behind the extraordinary life they lead.

If it were that easy, it's likely that all of us would live for more than ninety decades. On the other hand, the world is rife with a wide variety of diseases that can be traced back to things like food, chemicals, emissions, and lifestyle choices. We're far too engrossed in our work to be getting the regular exercise we need, and we don't have time to eat the proper amount of food that we require. There simply is not enough time to cultivate friendships and deepen existing social ties. Numerous contemporary cultures in the West center their identities on achievements that can be measured in terms of money and popularity. Okinawa is unique in that it is a place on earth where people enjoy better health and live longer lives than in almost any other place. The residents of this island believe that the secret to their continued existence lies in their ability to channel positive energies while simultaneously releasing any that may be detrimental to their goals. They have a long history of living a life filled with joy and accomplishment.

It is essential that the word "purposeful" be emphasized here. Even people who are retired get out of bed every day with a sense of purpose and a goal in mind for that day, regardless of how trivial or insignificant the goal may be. Okinawans are healthier and more physically fit than their Western counterparts in spite of the island's more rural and unforgiving environment as well as the limited access they have to modern medicine and health care. They do not suffer from conditions such as cancer, cardiovascular disease, diabetes, or psychological conditions such as depression or dementia.

On Okinawa, residents put all of their focus into cultivating deep and meaningful connections with one another. No one has to go through life alone and unattended because they have the support of their family and friends throughout their entire life. Those who are older help those who are younger, and even those who are younger help those who are older; both generations live together in a symbiosis that is upbeat and accepting. People who participate in these types of social networks feel a greater sense of calm and security in their day-to-day lives because they are aware that they can count on the support of others in the event that they require assistance of any kind. The diet of most Okinawans is lean, healthy, and light, consisting primarily of vegetables and tofu. They supplement their diet with a variety of soy foods in addition to eating well-balanced, low-carb foods. They are able to live a life that is well-rounded thanks to their diet.

They find that if they avoid meat, along with sugar, fats, and highly processed foods, they are better able to fight against cancer, diabetes, heart disease, and obesity. A significant component of the diet is fat-burning green tea. They also have a good supply of ginger, mugwort, many different kinds of herbs, and chili peppers. In addition to regularly engaging in sweet and healthy eating, Okinawan culture places a strong emphasis on physical activity. They incorporate activities such as walking, dancing, and gardening into their daily routines. They spend a significant amount of time breathing in the clean air and reaping the benefits of being exposed to the sun and the outdoors. They are safer, have stronger muscles, high vitamin levels, and generally possess happier moods as a result of their daily exposure to exercise and sunshine. In addition, they have higher vitamin levels.

Living on Okinawa is not like taking a stroll in the park. The people of Okinawa have mastered the art of putting the past in its proper place: in their tangled and murky history. On the other hand, they are concentrating on the uncomplicated pleasures that today has to offer. The lesson that we need to take away from this culture is that the quality of one's life should not be measured in terms of fame and wealth. Rather, we should make it a priority to improve the caliber of the interactions we have with one another, to discover inner calm in the most routine of activities, and to lead lives that are both upbeat and physically demanding.

Ikigai is a Japanese word that can be translated as "a person's purpose for living" or "your own internal motivation to go out of your house and carry out your job." It is believed that the islanders' ability to live off the land is due to their strong sense of ikigai. It's also possible to think of this as the intersection of four distinct aspects of your life: what you're passionate about, where your talents lie, how you can make a living, and what the world needs.

The majority of Japanese people believe that everyone has what they call a "ikigai," which can be translated as "destiny" or "calling." However, while some people are able to figure out their ikigai rather quickly, others require more time to arrive at this conclusion. If you are part of the second category, it is imperative that you keep going; after all, ikigai is what will ultimately inspire you to drag yourself out of bed when you are feeling too depressed to do so on your own.

The work that Okinawans produce is also of a very high quality. In their day-to-day work, they are extremely precise and place a significant amount of importance on paying close attention to the smallest of details.

For example, a professional craftswoman in a paintbrush mill in Okinawa is famous for her brushes because she spent her entire life perfecting the craft of attaching human hair to a brush. Her brushes are in high demand because of her dedication to the craft. Because she considers her work to be her life's calling, she is able to perform each task with a level of dexterity and expertise that is unmatched by her peers. If your ikigai is the line of work that you are currently engaged in, it is highly unlikely that you will ever retire. And if your ikigai is something like a hobby that brings you joy and a sense of calm, you should never, ever give up on that. Because Okinawans adhere to these values, they maintain a high level of physical activity well into their senior years.

When they are compelled to retire, they will nevertheless look for ways to continue being active in their communities, such as taking up gardening or some other form of alternative employment.

Chapter Twelve

Defining Ikigai

But how does one go about discovering their own ikigai? To get started, we need to learn the two different definitions of life and how each one influences us.

Love

The first and most important definition of life is love. Love is the highest and most important reason any of us should be here on this planet. No matter if we're looking for it from our own parents or a potential romantic partner, we never stop looking for it. Love can take many different forms, and depending on how it manifests itself in our lives, it may or may not be beneficial to us. One of the reasons that love is considered to be an essential component of life is due to the fact that it has the potential to characterize our very selves. When you love someone, you believe that you would do anything for them, including giving up your life. This belief provides you with purpose, and if you are a male, you may believe that the reason you were born was to protect the person you love the most in the world. But the problem with this is that love, when we don't understand what it really is, can also be problematic for us.

Love is not about the other person. You can't just assume that your entire identity is wrapped up in taking care of other people. What if that person is no longer in your life or changes their mind about being protected by you at some point? When people lose love in their life, it can cause them to act in extreme ways, and we have all heard horror stories about breakups that went horribly wrong. This occurs because the thing that caused you to fall in love with it was only fleeting and not permanent.

The kind of love that Ikigai discusses is a love that is not limited by time or location; it is a love that is universal. It's about falling deeply in love with who you are and understanding that you contain the entirety of the universe within you. Bear in mind that everything you see only exists because of you, even if you think that statement sounds trite. This indicates that the world does not exist outside of your own mind, and as a consequence, everything is, in some sense, a component of you.

The question now is, how do you figure out what it is that you genuinely adore? You absolutely must experiment with the Kondo method. Search through the things you own to identify the items that hold significant value for you. Consider that you have a car—what does that reveal about you? That you are able to make money? Is there any depth to that at all? The only way to find true love in your life is to look for those things that don't serve an immediate purpose but you keep them anyway. This is the only way to find it. How about an old photograph of you and your family; does something like that help you in any way? No. Therefore, why do you continue to cling to it? It is quite evident that the photograph is the thing that you value the most. You will be able to retrace your steps and determine what is meaningful to you and what is not by doing so.

Talent

Talent is the second meaning to be found in life. Not talent in the sense of being able to accomplish something, but rather what are you capable of producing. Because there isn't much else in the world that can tell us who we are besides ourselves, it can be challenging for us as human beings to figure out what the real point of our lives is. The majority of people will simply list their accomplishments in response to the question "who are you?" What gives with that? mainly due to the fact that we have a tendency to believe that the things we have accomplished are more real and substantial than we are. Because it tells us what we are good at creating and how that relates to who we are at our core, our talent helps bridge this gap.

What can we infer about certain individuals based on the fact that their singing abilities are well developed? That they should get a job and make a lot of money? The majority of people's response would be that, but those who truly appreciate singing are aware that it allows them to connect with their own inner feelings. It is a mode of expression that is particular to them only. People who draw art are able to create what they feel, which enables them to process their feelings more effectively. Painting is considered to be therapeutic because it enables us to express how we are truly feeling on the inside.

It's possible that you don't believe you have any talents, but this is probably because you haven't actively sought them out. Your special ability does not have to be something commonplace, such as singing, dancing, or painting. You can find happiness in anything, even if it's something as simple as sewing or just getting your house in order. You will know that something is a talent of yours when you not only feel like doing it even when you have nothing to do, but also feel like you're in a stride when you're doing it. It's almost as if you forget who you are in order to become one with the activity at hand. This way, you will be able to determine what it is that you feel connected to.

Ikigai and the Concept of Entrepreneurship

Since the beginning of time, the goal of every single human being has been to achieve a lifestyle that is both enjoyable and satisfying in some way. Outside of our own homes, we are looking for things to do that will make us happy and that can be done anywhere. We all have the desire to contribute to society in some way while also remaking the world in a manner that is congruent with our own perceptions of the world. According to the tenets of Japanese philosophical thought, the term "ikigai" does not refer to an activity that one can participate in outside of their place of employment in order to divert their attention from their responsibilities there. Rather, ikigai is viewed as something that ought to be present in each Because we spend a significant amount of time in our workplace, it can be challenging to feel at ease there, especially if we have to make a herculean effort each morning to drag ourselves out of bed and make our way to a location where we do not feel respected. It is the point at which we begin our individual journey with the world, and if it does not satisfy us, we may end up feeling disconnected from the world as a result. People in every company should always come first, even before the achievement of privately held ambitions such as financial success or public recognition. This should always be the case. This may sound immature, but the simple truth is that if you look after the well-being of your employees, your profits are likely to increase by a factor of ten. Investing in the intrinsic motivation of your workforce, also known as the ikigai of your entire team, can help increase profits.

When investigating the problem of locating a job that is suitable for one's needs, one will inevitably run into the concept of satisfaction. But in addition to that, there are a few other considerations that ought to be made. To help you decide where you want to work, you should educate yourself on the following factors:

There is trust between coworkers and leaders.

You should feel proud of the work that you are doing.

Working Together as a Team

If you want to grow and improve, the very first place that you need to start is with trust; it's the glue that holds the workforce together.

Through the relationship that exists between employee and employer, trust is built. If you are successful in establishing trust in your workplace, you will reap a plethora of benefits, including but not limited to the following: the employees in your workplace will demonstrate a more laid-back demeanor, everyone will have the perception that they can rely on each other for support, everyone will have the perception that they are valued, and everyone will become significantly more at ease when it comes to discussing their perspectives and ideas.

Pride and camaraderie are the most important things, but they are becoming less common every day. Because they are dependent on the characteristics of an individual and the requirements that they have, each of these values is experienced in a person's life in a manner that is unique to that person. They depend on the connection that the worker has with his or her job (pride) as well as the connection that the worker has with his or her coworkers (camaraderie). Personal and unique requirements must be met by each person's occupation in order for them to feel content, and it is of the utmost importance to place everyone in a position where they can realize their ambitions. The personalities and varied preferences of each individual, as well as their respective needs, determine the quality of the relationships that people have with their coworkers. It is essential for there to be camaraderie in the workplace that the management has the ability to easily match employees with coworkers who have similar interests and qualities.

When the concept of 'living and letting live' is considered, a connection can be made between ikigai and other values, such as pride and camaraderie. Even in situations where individuals are likely to disagree with one another, a harmonious working environment can be created by valuing one's own life purpose while also appreciating the life purposes of those around one.

Hope, pride, and camaraderie are the three factors that need to be addressed first in order for a company to develop a workforce that is filled with contented workers. Listening to your staff members and understanding the needs they have on the inside is the most effective way to create a happier work environment. If you are able to keep them happy, they will work hard to ensure the success of your company. Keep in mind that the things that other people are saying are more important than the things that you have to say because of this. It's a common misconception that leading others requires one to be dominant and take up as much space as possible in conversations and meetings, but this is not true. You should never forget the fact that as a leader, all you are doing is directing and supervising the work that others are doing. You don't do any work yourself, and you aren't the one who is creating value for the company. Your job is to pay attention to what they are saying; you should let other people speak as much as possible because doing so will provide you with additional insight into the manner in which they are feeling; consequently, you will be in a better position to assist them in improving their performance. You want your employees to be open with you about what they are thinking rather than keeping it a secret from you.

If you want other people to share their thoughts, the first thing you need to do is make them feel like they are welcome. Don't use your phone or your laptop, and try not to be constantly distracted by other people if you want the other person to feel comfortable expressing their feelings in that setting. Being a good listener also means getting to know your employees better; you can't expect to understand what someone means unless you know their personality, background, and the kind of person they are. As a leader, it is important to remember to interact with your employees on an equal plane and to share something about yourself as well. In this way, the personal connection you form will enhance the empathy quotient, and this will help you get the most out of your employees. It is also the best way to humanize people; if the purpose of leading people is to see them as a herd, the only way to counter that is by individualizing people. It is also the best way to humanize people. You have to see them not just as coworkers but as people with families, dreams, and a life outside of work.

You can only motivate people to work harder by making them feel like they are a part of the team, which is something that the majority of leaders tend to forget. Your employees will begin to feel a sense of pride in their work once you recognize the contributions they have made to the company and give them opportunities for advancement. Moreover, the most effective method for instilling a sense of pride in one's workforce is to provide opportunities for them to participate in activities that have personal significance. If you have an employee who is concerned about the health of the planet, you ought to give them the opportunity to work in an industry that is devoted to conserving natural resources. This will generate a motivation that will push them to work despite the fact that you are not paying them (although you must). In order to maintain a sense of solidarity within the workplace, it is necessary to ensure that everyone has the confidence to speak their mind without fear of being judged. It is important to convey to your employees, regardless of whether or not you are in a management position, that you think of them as members of your family. They shouldn't be afraid of you because that won't make them feel like they have a purpose; rather, it will demotivate them and make them feel helpless.

Chapter Thirteen

Locating your Ikigai

There are some people who claim that they are unable to find the fulfillment that they seek within their own personal capacities or thoughts. The majority of people have to suffer through the unpleasant experience of having to drag themselves painfully out of bed and out of the house in order to complete their daily responsibilities. Many of us have long since forgotten what it was like to go to work filled with enthusiasm and commitment to our work. People have a very difficult time igniting a spark of life in their work, and the concept of discovering their ikigai hasn't even had a chance to emerge as an option.

One of the primary takeaways from a study on ikigai was that it is impossible to achieve extrinsic motivation, or, to put it another way, it is unrealistic to try to motivate people with material things. According to the findings of scientists, individuals are only able to respond to inspiration that comes from within themselves. The pursuit of one's ikigai, or life's purpose, is at the heart of Japanese philosophical practice. When you think back on it, you'll realize that you probably had a strong preference for something when you were a kid. This will come to mind when you reflect on the past. Once we reach the age of maturity, who we become is dependent on socio-economic factors such as what we do, what our parents think we should do, and what kind of income we believe we need to achieve our ideal standards of living.

There is a set of four questions that you need to ask yourself in order to improve your daily orientation. When we are mired in the haze of everyday life, it can be difficult to recognize our own capabilities. There are four questions that may be able to assist us in locating our way. You can use them as a compass that leads you closer to your target if you write them down and put them in a location where you will frequently come across them. These questions are as follows: What is my role in the play that is my life? Do you consider yourself to be more of an extrovert or an introvert? Which of the two options—working on the project by yourself or with others—do you think you'll enjoy more? If it's a combination of the two, are you still going to enjoy the situation? Always make sure to write down your responses to these questions whenever you find a potential new location at which you can find a community and a place of employment.

Which activities bring me the most joy and satisfaction? When exactly did time begin to pass so quickly? What is something that you could do on purpose for a number of hours and not become bored with it? It is possible that this will be an activity in which you will feel completely involved and in which you will not feel the urge to give up.

Which types of jobs are the easiest for you to perform? Is there something that comes naturally to you but that other people appear to have difficulty with? The vast majority of people in today's world find it very easy to organize documents in an uncomplicated manner, while others are exceptional at taking into consideration a variety of points of view.

You need to discover what you are naturally talented at doing.

What was it that you looked forward to doing the most when you were a child? This query contributes to the foundation of your ikigai. Was the activity something that appealed to you on an intrapersonal, psychological, moral, physical, linguistic, aural, or possibly even a visual level? You will gain a better understanding of the sense of experience to which you are predisposed as a result of this.

Ikigai is the point at which one's life's four most important facets—passion, one's vocation, career, and daily routine—converge. To put it another way, the goal that we are all working toward is to locate the ideal location that exemplifies the ideal combination of each of these four components. A location that brings together everything that you adore with the things that you excel at, accommodates the things that you treasure most about yourself, and has a deeper significance that links you to the greater meaning of the universe. Ikigai can only be finished if the purpose you find entails some kind of helping others or giving back to the community. This occurs due to the fact that we almost always feel more at ease giving gifts than receiving them. After you have determined each of these components, the next step is to begin with your compass. Get started on putting together your questions, and check to see if there is anything that fits in with your answers.

Chapter Fourteen

Other Ways That Kaizen Can Be Used

The concept of kaizen is not limited to the realm of business; rather, it is one that is applicable to a significant portion of one's life. In this chapter, we're going to talk about how the Kaizen theory can assist you in various facets of your own personal life.

Personal Development

In addition to the organizational philosophy that underpins Kaizen, the concept of Kaizen encompasses a much broader range of topics than those that are typically addressed in business settings. It is commonly believed that everyone has a built-in motivation to strive to improve themselves in some way, shape, or form. By exposing workers to a variety of concepts and strategies, Kaizen helps them develop the skills necessary for personal advancement. It enables them to evaluate their lives by comparing them to predetermined standards of physical, social, emotional, and psychological existence and, where applicable, to make suggestions for how those standards can be met more effectively. The majority of participants in this adventure have expressed a preference for concentrating their efforts on methods that involve taking a series of relatively simple steps that will ultimately make their lives simpler.

When a person first begins to engage in Kaizen practices, the majority of the behaviors they want to improve are of a physical nature.

These behaviors may include sleep, exercise, and diet. If these new behaviors are adopted, then they will be motivated to proceed to the self-improvement stage where the emphasis will be placed on their emotional facets.

Any employee who participates in the Kaizen initiatives will notice an improvement in their behavior, and every day that passes will feel like a happier day for them. Their exercise routine, diet, and even their quality of sleep will all benefit from this change. They will also begin to exhibit behaviors that are more complex in relation to their interpersonal skills and even their spiritual commitments. They will also be able to adopt a Kaizen mentality in their private lives, which will allow them to reap the many benefits of this philosophy in every other facet of their lives.

The process of transition is often described as one that never ends. If a person has been successful in a particular area of their life, they will be encouraged to apply the same strategies they used to achieve that success to other areas of their lives. Individuals find it much simpler to change their behaviors as a result of the Kaizen theory, which encourages them to establish short-term, long-term, and intermediate-term goals and to focus on making incremental improvements as they move closer to achieving those goals. Once Kaizen is implemented, the requirement to be successful in multiple fields in addition to one does not go away. Because of this, advocacy for the acceptance of the theory of continuous improvement is strongly encouraged. When attempting to change behaviors, it is essential to keep in mind that not all behaviors are inherently unhealthy or have a negative influence on one's wellbeing in some way. The nature of our relationship with our routines is what determines whether or not they are beneficial to us. They are required in order for us to be able to work on some level each and every day. Our unfavorable emotions have the potential to be transformed into positive ones; these are the emotions that, when we are feeling depleted and stressed, can be used to help us feel more secure and supported. It can be challenging to break free from the comfort zone that our routines provide, and as a result, we often prefer to go about our daily lives as though we were some kind of automaton.

You might be curious about the reasons why changing habits is so challenging. Did you know that repetitive actions save a lot of time and energy for us? When it comes to making changes to them, it may appear frightening and intimidating because they function as sedatives that calm us down by recreating familiarity. In order for there to be a shift in the repetitive habits that we engage in, the first step is to learn how we initially got socialized into such behavior. The next step that you need to take is to address the patterns by identifying the factors that result in undesirable behaviors. You need to be aware of the incentives that we frequently receive momentarily from engaging in such behavior, in addition to knowing the trigger that causes these habits. Think about how such incentives influence our future actions because we want to achieve the same level of success in the future, and how modifying these routines can lead to the achievement of more long-term goals and rewards.

Your following question will probably be, "How long does this shift last?" The amount of time that it takes for an individual to reach a state of automatic processing varies greatly from person to person. It depends on the person, the environment they were raised in, and the person's attitude toward change in their own life and the world around them. To be able to break old habits, one needs to learn new ones in a manner that involves gradually stepping up the level of intensity of the connection between the individual's current circumstances and the habit that is being performed. The more often a pattern is repeated, the greater the likelihood that it will become ingrained.

Dietary Habits

Those who want to improve their relationship with food and their attitude toward it may find it helpful to apply Kaizen strategies to their eating routine. You shouldn't try to restrict or eliminate the enjoyment you get from eating; rather, you should focus on making minor adjustments to the way you consume food in order to cultivate a healthy mentality and improve both your mind and body. Let's take a look at how Kaizen can transform your current eating habits into three distinct dietary goals: goals for the short term, the medium term, and the long term.

Drink More Water

The amount of water that you should consume on a daily basis is determined by a variety of factors, including your gender, the foods that you typically consume, the number of workouts that you perform, and the surrounding environment. Milk, coffee, tea, and other sugar-free beverages can be beneficial additions to a diet, and drinking water is not going to hurt you in any way. There are a lot of people who forget to drink water, but with the introduction of Kaizen, it will become a habit, and it will therefore be beneficial to the body even if you forget to drink it. Remember to pay attention to the water requirements of your body, and make sure to drink water at regular intervals. You should avoid drinking an excessive amount of water because it could be harmful to the body.

At the present time, there are a significant number of people living on our planet who consume meat. There are indisputable medical advantages to be gained from consuming less meat overall, particularly red meat. Because it is a gradual process of enhancement, the Kaizen method is ideally suited for this kind of transition. The only thing you need to do is make a gradual transition and start eating more vegetables and fruits. The consumption of vegetables is highly valued in the traditional diet of Japan. This diet is not only more affordable, but it also provides your body with all of the nutrients that it could possibly require.

The practice of Kaizen is an excellent strategy for enhancing one's diet with more fresh fruits and vegetables. As a vegan, you need to limit the amount of sugar you consume. It is commonly believed that consuming a lot of sugar and soft drinks is extremely risky, and while this may be true to some extent, it is not entirely accurate. So, remember to stop drinking fizzy drinks. Even though the fruits you continue to consume as part of your Kaizen implementation contain only natural sugars, this does not mean that you can eliminate all sugar from your diet completely. You should begin by cutting back on the typical amount of sugar that you consume; first, just reduce it by half, and then gradually eliminate it from your diet altogether because the process is gradual. It takes some time for your body to become accustomed to a new source of energy, such as natural sugars, and that adjustment period is necessary. Cereals contain added sugar that has been preserved in a way that is harmful to your body, so you should avoid eating them. Additionally, you should stop adding sugar to hot drinks like coffee and tea.

Reduce the Amount of Food You Consume Daily

This is in relation to decreasing the quantity of food that you consume. Because we don't measure our food based on the appropriate portions, we have a tendency to consume more food than is healthy for us. After you have finished preparing and eating your meal, check to see that there are no leftovers, and keep track of how hungry you are throughout the process.

Eat While Paying Attention

Maintain your concentration on, and get as much pleasure out of, every bite you take. At meals, make an effort to eat with as few interruptions as possible; turn off the television and avoid eating in front of a laptop or other electronic device. Instead of placing orders for food and other items from outside sources, you should focus on preparing the meals. We are left with a feeling of hunger if we do not pay attention to the food that we are eating. This is because we did not really enjoy the food that we ate, but rather we just ended up swallowing it down. Therefore, even when your stomach is full, you continue to have the desire to eat, which is the primary factor that contributes to excessive eating.

Mindset

Your mental disposition and temperament are either the greatest asset or the greatest barrier that stands between you and the accomplishment of your goals. Regardless of how hard we try to get rid of our internal issues, they continue to cast a shadow over our capabilities and strengths. Because of this, even when we are fully capable of accomplishing our goals, we frequently have difficulty doing so. Changing your mindset is not something that can be accomplished in a single day. After years of experience, your convictions, ideals, and behaviors have become ingrained in you. It has taken a lot of time and effort over the years for those poor habits and assumptions to mesh perfectly with your personality. But as soon as you accepted them, they started controlling how you conducted yourself. Therefore, in order to replace those poor habits and erroneous values with healthy habits and correct beliefs, it will require a persistent and positive improvement in your day-to-day persona. Fortunately, Kaizen is going to assist you with carrying out this mission.

Chapter Fifteen

The Process of Coming to Understand Yourself

Getting to know oneself is the first step in the process, which is where it all begins. You need to put in the effort to improve your routines by working with Kaizen, and you can learn more about your behaviors by keeping a daily log of your attitude. You should be able to learn how and why you react to certain situations in the way that you are, such as reacting with anger and stress when your Internet connection goes down. For example: As time goes on, it is my hope that you will be able to cultivate the ability to control and keep tabs on your feelings.

Altering your Beliefs and Opinions

Your beliefs and principles will prevent you from making a change in your life that is for the better. Despite the fact that a positive change challenges the negative views you currently hold, it is less likely that you will accept the change in your life unless you change the way you think about it. If you have the mindset that yoga is an ineffective form of exercise, the likelihood of you using yoga as a form of physical therapy to heal your body is close to zero. You are unable to bring about meaningful change so long as you hold a negative belief that runs counter to a positive action. It is because of this obstacle that the life-altering power of Kaizen cannot yet be fully realized.

You can create little beliefs incrementally through the use of the Kaizen method, just as you can use it to develop little habits incrementally. An individual who lacks confidence in something may end up developing a habit by employing the power of a positive belief in that something. If you don't believe that you will have the stamina to run just seven miles, then you should begin by convincing yourself that you can run for three miles. Do you think you'll be able to run for seven miles if you believe that and if you achieve that level of physical exertion? Do not believe that Kaizen can make any number of things possible that cannot currently be done. You will learn through kaizen that everything is attainable if you just take things one step at a time and make incremental improvements.

When we see evidence, our beliefs alter. If you practice yoga regularly and find that it improves your health, there is no way you can dispute the validity of the claim that yoga is a healing art. As a result of the fact that the purpose of kaizen is to demonstrate to the unconscious mind on a consistent basis through seemingly insignificant evidence that it is effective, the transitions that it brings about are typically of a measured and gradual nature. Nevertheless, it has the potential to change who you are and what you value in a fundamental way.

Altering your Typical Routines

There are certain patterns of behavior that we all exhibit, and these help to determine how we react to various occurrences in our environment. Alterations to the conditions of our surroundings set in motion these predetermined patterns. The ability to find the bright side of a challenging circumstance,

the growth of personal agency in the face
of adversity, and the preservation of people's
dignity in all circumstances are all examples of
positive social movements. Yet other patterns
of behavior, such as becoming agitated
when confronted with a stressful situation,
completely losing faith in something, ignoring
essential tasks, and disregarding connections,
are all undesirable. In a situation in which
someone's life is in danger, one person
might feel energised, while another might feel
overwhelmed with fear. This is the reason
why some people look for excitement in
their lives while others look for security and
predictability. It will be difficult for someone
who is looking for a healthy environment to
leave their town or nation in the hope of finding
a better job and living a better life. Changing
your entire position in life is a significant
undertaking, and the prospect of doing so can

induce fear in some people. These potentially terrifying scenarios can be made less of a concern with Kaizen by first being broken down into their component parts.

Envision yourself participating in something that forces you out of your comfort zone or in a situation that leaves you feeling terrible and helpless. Maybe you're good at elocution or skydiving. No matter the circumstance, this holds true. By challenging our comfort zones, we strengthen our character and develop our resilience. As an example, if you're preparing for a big move to a new city, you might try visualizing what it will be like to live there. You can also visit the city frequently to get used to the new setting. The point is to prevent your mind from going into overdrive trying to figure everything out. You can decide how you'll respond by managing your anxiety. There is no challenge too great to overcome; what matters most is how you handle adversity when it arises.

With the Kaizen method of incremental improvement, you can avoid burnout by focusing on small, manageable steps rather than the entire project at once. It's best to break down a daunting task into smaller, more manageable chunks and focus on those until your anxiety levels drop. Then, and only then, proceed to the next part of that scenario.

Personal Time Management

For most people, scheduling their personal time is a major challenge. The standard 24-hour day doesn't seem like nearly enough time to complete all of your daily responsibilities. It's not about how many hours you have, but rather how you allocate them. Learning how to better manage one's time is a skill that is essential to success in any endeavor, whether at work or at home, as well as to the pursuit of a higher standard of living in general.

If you're looking for ways to free up more time in your schedule, the Kaizen method can help. Make a list of everything crucial that needs to be done this week. These can range from routine, daily chores to steps necessary to reach a larger, more ambitious objective. Write down all the time-wasting activities in which you tend to overindulge afterward. Examples of such routines include sitting in front of the television, playing video games, or sleeping. But with Kaizen's help, you don't have to give up all your annoying habits at once. Your best bet is to replace each negative habit with one good one, one step at a time. Cut your TV time by 20 minutes a day, and use that extra time for a walk or some creative thinking. The goal is to free up time that can then be spent on more healthful activities.

Attaining Perfection Within Oneself

Describe the best possible version of yourself. If you try to solve this issue by looking inward, you may experience a revelation about what you value most in life. Each of us has an ideal version of ourselves that we hope to one day become. One's ideal self can be of any personality type, from eminent to lowly. It's possible that you'll begin to identify with a movie character you've seen many times. Whatever the case may be, most of us never quite arrive at our ideal selves, but that doesn't stop us from striving for them. And while the pinnacle of self-actualization will always elude us, the Kaizen approach can give us a way of life that promotes constant change, bringing us closer to this imagined identity.

With Kaizen, you focus on improving one aspect of your character at a time. The question of how to gain self-assurance, for instance, is a common one. Most people's assurance is proportional to their level of wealth. However, if your bank balance stays the same, your self-assurance will remain stagnant as well. Turn your attention elsewhere. There's a chance that money will always be a stressful factor in your life. If you're going to put your faith in something, might as well put it in something that will last. You might be the life of the party because of your infectious personality, your extensive knowledge of politics, or your musical prowess. Learn to see your skill as the ultimate source of your self-assurance, whatever it may be. Then stop thinking that your identity is established by how much money you have.

Experiment by going out into the world while dressed casually and carrying only a minimal amount of cash. You should network by becoming involved in conversations that have nothing to do with money. However, be honest about your financial situation right away and keep track of how people react. You will discover that most people do not base their opinion of you on such trivia. People who only care about you because of your wealth are not worth your time.

Cost Reduction

Every one of us is in this for the money. Money is the universal measuring stick for success because it buys us safety, self-assurance, and peace of mind. People are enamored with the concept and will go to any lengths to obtain some financial gain. There is no fast track to financial success. People's minds automatically go to more materialistic goals when they consider the prospect of financial success, such as owning a nicer home, driving a nicer car, and having a larger bank balance. The lessons of Kaizen show us that the best opportunities to cut costs lie in the smallest details. While putting away money gradually over time may not sound appealing, it is the most effective strategy for building wealth over time.

We are wasting a lot of money without even realizing it. Why? Because we waste money without considering its impact. You can turn saving money into a habit once you begin to notice and appreciate the little things that contribute to your financial well-being. Since Kaizen is predicated on incremental improvements, you should first consider how you can cut costs this week, and then this month and next year. Check your spending and see where your money is going the fastest out the door. You can improve in the following ways:

Charge Cards

Credit cards are a con because they give the false impression of financial security, encouraging you to spend more and more until you eventually max out your card and discover that your supposed wealth was an illusion. A common piece of advice from financial experts is to cut up your credit cards and never use them again. This is because credit cards condition us to view money as something easily obtained rather than something that requires effort and time. Most people don't have money, but they all act as if they do because they all carry a lot of debt and a false sense of security. Debt consolidation loans are the quickest way to pay off your credit card balances. Get rid of the card and convert the balance to a loan you can repay over time. Or you could just pull yourself together, put on your work boots, and get to paying down that debt.

Phone

Everyone has a secret desire to own the latest and greatest smartphone because of the aspirational quality it exudes. Do you really need to upgrade to the newest model of the same phone because it has a few extra bells and whistles? It turns out that the answer is negative. There's no sense going into debt and going hungry every month so you can afford a more expensive phone with a better camera. Additional charges add up quickly on a phone bill. You should do what you can to reduce recurring expenses, such as your data plan.

Food

As a group, we enjoy putting money toward culinary experiences. It's not easy to avoid spending on that one meal at your favorite restaurant, even when money is tight. The first step is obvious: give up eating at restaurants. The amount of times you eat out should be reduced even if you are compelled to do so by your job and social commitments. Restrict your food spending to a set number of days each week. A better strategy is to get up early every day and prepare food that will keep you going through your workday. Therefore, you won't have to waste time and money finding a suitable alternative to eating at home during lunch.

Smarter grocery shopping is something to consider as well. Get your supplies for the month all at once. Find the grocery store with the lowest prices and the best deals near you. The vast majority of people are too sluggish to change their habits, so they overlook these elementary considerations. It could take up to half an hour longer to get to a cheaper but more distant grocery store. But in the long run, you'll be able to save money, so it's a good idea to do it.

Subscriptions These days, everybody pays for Netflix, Hulu, and Amazon without giving much thought to how much money they're actually spending. If there are any recurring costs that you don't feel are absolutely necessary, you should stop paying them. To what extent do you require their services? Is it possible to find an option besides such a subscription? A Netflix subscription could be quite expensive, but if you and a friend or coworker split the cost, you could end up saving a significant amount of money by the end of the year.

Electricity

Because energy appears to be a limitless resource, most of us don't bother to monitor how much we use. Because of the excessive energy used for heating and cooling, you can cut your monthly electricity bills in half simply by turning off your heater or air conditioner when it is not in use. The simple act of turning off lights and unplugging appliances when they are not in use can have a significant impact. It's puzzling that the majority of people turn on their lights when they could just sit in the sun. Each little decision you make can have a significant impact over time, so it's important to think things through carefully.

There's no need to make all these changes at once, and some of them may be too much for you to handle. Keep trying until you find what works for you; there are opportunities to cut costs every day; all it takes is making one smart decision at a time until it becomes second nature. Don't throw away your hard-earned savings on frivolous purchases or unnecessary improvements to your home if you manage to accumulate any. Your money needs to start reproducing as soon as possible, so you need to start saving and investing.

Investing

If you're like most people, you dread the end of each pay period because it means you'll have less money to put toward your bills. The anxiety of missing even a single day of work can be debilitating, and it can have serious consequences for your physical and mental health. Start putting money away now so you'll have a safety net for the future and no longer have to worry about money worries. In addition to helping you solve your financial problems, this will give you peace of mind. You can't become wealthy through investment overnight like in the movies; it's a process that takes time. Finding a safe and stable financial instrument to invest in over time is all that's required.

After a while, you might even forget that you've been putting money away; however, over time, that small amount will grow into a sizeable sum that will serve you well in times of need.

You have complete freedom in deciding how to allocate your funds; you can invest in stocks, mutual funds, or even a simple savings account if you so choose. Never put money into the market without first thoroughly educating yourself on the subject. If you can't afford to pay for the advice of a financial expert, then look for information online. Before dropping any cash, make sure you've done your homework. Don't waste time and money trying to copy it, though. First, invest a small amount; then, once you've established your comfort level with the investment, gradually increase the amount you're putting in.

The financial strain from investing can be substantial. The best course of action is to take stock of your financial resources and the outlook for their continued stability. This will show you whether or not you have the financial wherewithal to engage in financial speculation. It's not wise to put too much of your income into the stock market if you have a job where your salary is subject to frequent changes. An unexpected increase in income allows you to increase your investment accordingly. The first step in investing is assessing your current financial standing and making a plan moving forward based on that. Look at your income every month and put away

5 percent more if it goes up, and skip investing altogether if it goes down. Patience is what Kaizen really wants from you. Be patient and only make small, incremental changes to your investment strategy, even if they are spaced out by months. This will increase your potential for profit while decreasing the risk you take. Because investing is a game in its own right, one must constantly be on the lookout for profitable opportunities.

Health

If you want to live a healthy life, mastering the Kaizen method is a must. You've probably told yourself a thousand times that this will be the time you finally start eating better and healthier. You probably wanted to stop smoking and drinking because you knew it would help you feel better physically and mentally. But it seems like nothing has helped so far. For the most part, this is because your goal is too lofty, and the two-hour exercise routine video you tried to follow every day was too taxing to maintain. The good news is that Kaizen can help you learn how to improve your health gradually, without overwhelming your brain or body.

The health benefits of losing even a small amount of weight and adopting healthier habits are substantial. The risk of developing diabetes, heart disease, and high cholesterol is reduced with regular, moderate exercise of just 20 minutes per day. Since Kaizen is an all-encompassing methodology, its positive effects on one's quality of life are inextricably linked to slimming down and working out. Let's say, like everyone else, you want to shed twenty pounds. It's easy to become a large target if you don't exercise at all. Therefore, you can divide the total into weekly goals that are more manageable, such as losing two pounds. This way, instead of expecting immediate results, you can give yourself ten weeks to reach your target. After settling on a weekly objective, you'll need to implement some minor Kaizen adjustments to reach your goal. You can find four examples below:

Everyday weigh-ins

Having this simple ritual will serve as a daily reminder of your weight. Studies have shown that people who keep track of their weight daily are more likely to engage in healthy behaviors, making weight loss a lot less of a struggle. In order to prepare for a workout and a healthy diet, you should make this a routine. This ritual will motivate you to start working out and eating healthier. When you see that your weight is lower than it was the day before, your brain will associate that with a positive emotion of satisfaction. You'll feel motivated to stick to your healthy eating and exercise plan.

Chapter Sixteen

Greater Posture

Just how much of your day is spent sitting? Most people sit at their desks for nine to thirteen hours a day, depending on their jobs and personal preferences. A select few actually find the drive to go out and purchase a standing desk.

Instead, try getting up from your seat and moving around for a few minutes about every half an hour. Get some fresh air by taking a short walk around the premises, or just stretch. Then, it's back to business as usual.

After practicing for two minutes, try increasing the time to four minutes. People who sit for long periods of time at work may benefit from finding small ways to increase the amount of time they stand throughout the day. If you spend a lot of time in front of the TV or a video game, this also applies to you. If you find yourself sitting for long periods of the day, try getting up and moving around the room during commercial breaks. You can make significant improvements to your health and way of life by adopting just a few of these practices.

Make Your Way Up the Steps

There are stairs in your building, whether it's an apartment complex, an office building, or both. You should keep using them. If the number of stairs leading to your office is too great for you to tackle all at once, you can always take the elevator down to ground level and then use the remaining flights to get to work. Keep adding new levels of stairs over the next few weeks. In order to achieve your goals, you should gradually increase your weekly step count. A few months from now, you might be surprised to see how much you've improved; in the meantime, you'll probably still vividly recall how exhausted you felt on those first few flights.

Put Your Car Farther Away From Your Intended Location

This is something that can be done wherever you take your car. Always park at a spot that is a little further away from where you need to go. By doing so, you'll get some much-needed exercise while traveling to and from each location. A weekly total of 20 minutes of walking can be achieved by simply walking through a parking lot for 3 minutes.

Whether your goal is to maintain a healthy weight or prevent illness, a healthy diet is an essential part of your daily routine. Most people today are aware that they can prepare a wide variety of healthy meals without leaving the house. However, incorporating the right foods into your daily routine and altering long-standing habits can be challenging. Kaizen can be useful when confronting this phobia.

Chapter Seventeen

Some suggestions for a well-rounded Kaizen diet

Daily Record of Food Consumption

Write down everything you eat and drink every day. You can keep track of the food you eat and the number of calories you consume with this tool. Now circle in green all the nutritious foods on the list, such as the vegetable salad, grains, greens, eggs, and so on. Draw pizza, cake, fatty foods, sugary drinks, alcoholic beverages, and other unhealthy food items with a red pen to emphasize their negative effects. Compare the number of green items to the number of red items on your list. Has the color red taken over your list?

The goal, from a Kaizen point of view, is to gradually enhance our eating routines until our journal is filled with green marks and contains fewer red marks. The plan is to gradually improve our diet by switching out just one unhealthy food item per week for a healthier option. Green tea can be used as a suitable alternative to soda. If you eat a slice of pizza, try subbing in a serving of vegetables the next time you eat.

Consume fewer calories.

Every time you eat, reduce your portion size by a little bit and rate how satisfied you are with your hunger on a scale from 1 to 10. The target score range is from 7 to 8. As a result, you calm down, but you still feel slightly peckish after every meal. It's because your brain needs some processing time to catch up with the fact that your body has just eaten. This means that the satiety sensation won't be released for several minutes. If you have a habit of overeating at meals like breakfast or dinner, try cutting back on your portion sizes gradually until you feel satisfied with a smaller amount of food.

Involvement in a Physical Activity

Maintaining a healthy lifestyle and physical fitness requires regular exercise. Whether your focus is on weight loss, muscle gain, or maintaining a healthy BMI, Kaizen can help you succeed at any type of physical activity. The most difficult part of starting a new exercise routine is finding the motivation to do so. The effort that we know something will require from us makes it difficult to begin. Getting into the habit of going to the gym regularly can be challenging, especially in the beginning. The average person fails to make it through the first week of their gym membership. People never fully commit to fitness because they are afraid of failing and also because they miss their old, sedentary ways of life. Using the Kaizen approach to exercise will help you immensely if you are experiencing similar difficulties. Some suggestions for getting going are as follows.

Keep tabs on how often you're exercising each day.

It's not enough to simply join the closest gym; physical training is the goal. Little bursts of physical activity, such as going for a five-minute walk, stretching your body (after every few hours spent in front of a computer), and taking the stairs instead of the elevator, can fill a lot of time. Regardless of the activities you choose, it is essential that you perform them on a daily basis. The primary goal of our Kaizen monitoring is to increase our average daily physical activity by small amounts. It's important to remember that the amount of time spent working on Kaizen each day is secondary to the fact that the work done today was even marginally better than the work done yesterday.

Workouts at the beginning and end of the day are ideal.

The average person has only two truly free hours per day. This is the time of day when we first open our eyes in the morning and when we lay our heads down for the night. Both of these times are great for squeezing in quick but effective workouts. Gentle exercises, such as back, leg, and shoulder stretches, are ideal for these times. And, just stroll around; stretch your torso out by bending at the waist and your hands by rotating them. A healthy habit is formed over time, and this is why establishing a morning or evening routine can have such a positive impact on your life. In addition, you won't have to worry about any physical exertion to begin or end your day. In order to start and end each day feeling refreshed and revitalized, regular exercise is essential because it allows the body to release built-up stress and tension.

Choose an Activity That Will Challenge Your Body

It's okay if intense forms of physical activity, like lifting weights, aren't your thing. There are other ways to incorporate variety into your regular workout routine. Think about getting together with a group of people who share your interest in dancing, hiking, or other fun outdoor activities.

Sports like tennis and soccer, in which extra movement is required, are great options. The most important thing is that you are making a concerted effort every day to get your body moving so that you can burn off calories rapidly. Introduce these new pursuits into your life gradually, just as you would any other Kaizen-related task. You can choose multiple activities and commit to them on a weekly basis, for instance. Kick off your weekend with a jog in the park, go on a hike every weekend, and plan an adventure trip once every three months with your pals.

Relationships

In all our interactions with others, whether romantic, professional, or otherwise, we strive for openness and truthfulness. The idea of "a good relation" is a complete fabrication in many of our minds. So, we do what we can to make it work and not let the little things stress us out. We work to maintain a peaceful partnership for as long as we can. But the little things keep piling up and many of our relationships are ruined in the process. Could something be done to stop this from happening? Is there anything we can do to stop all of our connections from deteriorating? Fortunately, Kaizen can help with that, too. There are two primary causes of relationship problems that lead to the development of resentment and the subsequent loss of positive recollections. To begin with, you and the other party never had a real conversation about the issues at hand, and you never even bothered to officially register your complaints. In addition, you realize that your own interpersonal skills aren't adequate to resolve the conflict through dialogue. Discussions can be productive, but only if we are all on the same page. There's no way for anyone to understand how you feel if you never express your emotions.

Many times, our conception of what constitutes a "good relationship" is based on ideals that are neither specific nor accurate. Maybe you believe that your life is a fairy tale just waiting to happen when you meet the right person. Or perhaps you believe that the other person contains a great manager who will value your input and treat you with the respect you deserve at the workplace. These generalizations can be found in any type of relationship. But the reality is that no romantic partnership can live up to our wildest fantasies. Sometimes what starts out as the perfect relationship turns into something much more complicated and trying for both people involved. And that's only natural; evolution forces change in all of us. Depending on our experiences, we can mature into better or worse people. In any relationship, you need to put forth regular effort. The essence of Kaizen is the realization that perfection is unattainable but that progress toward it is possible through small, steady steps. This is a truth of life that you must acknowledge. Since it is a universal truth that all things evolve and change over time, you must accept that it is necessary to allow for some degree of personal growth and change in any relationship you have. Every relationship, from that with your spouse to that with your coworkers, is built on a foundation of tenacity and teamwork in the face of repeated setbacks.

Here's how to fix a relationship that's grown too complicated:

Consider the relationship you find most trying at the moment and make a list of all the things that annoy you about it. List the positive things you bring to the relationship. In addition, list all the negative things you've done to the relationship - You didn't seem to have time for your spouse; were you both too busy? Is he or she trying to get you to commit more time to the family?

Now, write down all the things you feel like your partner has done wrong in the relationship.

Do something about your weekly slip-ups. If you want to make sure you spend quality time with your family, you can use a mobilealert to remind you to do things like call your spouse at lunchtime or play with the kids after dinner. These subtle shifts in how you act every day will not go unnoticed by your significant other and may even motivate them to give more attention to themselves. Relationships are two-way streets; if you want the other person to change, you have to be willing to change for them first.

However, if you continue to feel that your partner is treating you in an abhorrent way, it is time to seek an alternative form of patching things up, as we will cover in the following section.

Maintain a Healthy "I" and "We" Ratio

The ratio of "I" to "We" changes all the time depending on the nature of your relationship. A strong relationship is measured by the "We" you use to refer to one another. Your ability to maintain your individuality within the context of the relationship is what the "I" measures. An unhealthy amount of "I" can damage even the strongest of relationships, even if it's just a casual friendship or a professional one. Relationships are more challenging to manage when they involve an excessive amount of "We." In what amounts might it become dangerous? That is something that should be discussed between you and your significant other. It's important to strike a balance between "I" and "We" in all of your interactions. Your shared emotions need not overpower your individuality. No one should ever feel they need to totally forget who they are in a relationship.

When and How to Fight

A part of any human connection is the inevitable presence of disagreement, dispute, and debate. You may be able to control the scale and intensity of your fights, but you cannot eliminate conflict entirely. Mastering the skill of fighting fairly is the most effective strategy for resolving conflicts. Everyone wants a conflict to end with justice, but that can only happen if both sides work to resolve the issue at hand rather than simply settle the score. Love, loyalty, and integrity are the cornerstones of a productive discussion that leads to mutual understanding and agreement. You wouldn't be fighting if you didn't care about each other, so in a way, love even includes conflict. The fight itself would be a waste of time and effort if you didn't give a damn about the other person.

Just how does one go about having a civilized argument? Regrettably, we tend to feel most comfortable and to lose our temper the quickest in our closest relationships. This occurs when we feel safe enough with another person to show every side of our personality, even the ugly ones. That's why conflicts with loved ones, whether romantic, parental, or social, can escalate rapidly. The goal of the Kaizen method in romantic relationships is to make it second nature to show affection and gratitude, even in the midst of conflict. Look for ways to fill your arguments with words that show your appreciation and love for one another while still making your point. If you feel like blaming the other person, remind them that you love them and that your respect for them will not diminish if they accept responsibility for their actions.

An easy way to get people to see things your way is to express your love and admiration for them. By taking into account the other person's perspective, this tactic immediately reduces the tenor of an argument. You'll need to take it slow with those who have self-centered personality styles if you want to achieve this level of understanding. Kaizen methodology is useful in this situation. If you find yourself in an argument with another person, try to reduce the amount of time spent placing blame and maximize the time spent showing respect. Proper and sincere use of words like "love" and "respect" will ease tensions for everyone involved. When you say these words to the other person during an argument, you are reminded of your shared humanity and are more likely to tune in to what they have to say. The person you're in a committed relationship with will be prompted to hear you out as well.

Communication

Communicating with one person is not the same as communicating with another, and this varies from relationship to relationship. Some friends and close family members may be close enough for you to share your deepest thoughts and feelings with them, while your relationship with others may be more surface level. How close we get with others and who we let peer into our private lives is a function of how much we trust them. At the same time, it is dependent on the level of trust others place in us. Each new couple enters into this agreement when they first start dating. A more positive and open atmosphere for communication with the people in your life can be fostered by following the advice provided below.

Where do you feel pain?

Similar to other Kaizen methods, this one starts with introspection. Relationships suffer when you turn into a distant or unapproachable person. The point is to recognize when you've experienced a shift in your emotions due to one of the triggers that causes you to withdraw or put up barriers that prevent you from connecting with others.

Think back on a time when you had a heated argument with someone you disagreed with. Which specific words or phrases most irritated you? Jot down all of those terms on a piece of paper and keep a file of them. Notice the people and things in your daily life that trigger anxious thoughts and feelings. This research will show you how you aren't as logical as you'd like to think you are. You'll develop an awareness of the places, people, ideas, and circumstances that trigger your tendency to harden up and withdraw. Ideally, you'll grow a new level of self-awareness that will help you control your emotional responses. You can use your list as a tool to learn more about the emotional and cognitive processes that underlie your responses to varying situations.

Dealing with Abusers

To some, relationships are nothing more than a means to an end, a means to get what they want. No matter how suffocated or horrible the other person may feel, their only concern is satisfying their own needs. They are assertive, conceited, and manipulative in their relationships with others in order to achieve their goals. Tackling such men can be challenging because they lack an understanding of love, reverence, and dignity. Managing these types of people requires introspection on your part to determine why you continue to spend time with them. To keep your self-respect intact, you must constantly remind yourself that any relationship in which your independence is being compromised is not worthy of your continued participation.

Avoiding these people is the most effective way to cut them out of your life. However, it is often necessary for us to keep up these connections, whether it be for professional or familial reasons. When confronted by hostile individuals, it's helpful to have a repertoire of responses at the ready.

See if you can sit quietly with your eyes closed and have a conversation with an angry mental image of yourself. Let your mind wander to something they've said that has you seething with rage. Do you sense that they have some control over you? Do you find yourself unable to approach them because of your fears?

Think about responding to various arguments. It's kind of like conditioning your mind to say whatever it can so that you can ignore the person's hostile attitude and get your point across when the time comes.

Defend yourself as forcefully and confidently as you can from this assault. With such people, you must be firm and unyielding. If someone is asking for your sympathy, you should investigate to determine if they are telling the truth.

You can't connect with others and build meaningful relationships if you lack the patience to listen and comprehend what they're saying. Listening gives you insight into other people's mental processes, emotional states, and worldviews. The ability to listen and comprehend is the key to successfully navigating challenging situations. To truly listen means to look past the other person's pretenses. You need to practice actively listening to other people in order to develop this skill. When we listen, we take in more than just the words that are being spoken. Body language, tone, and the emphasis placed on particular words are all part of this. Humans have a bias toward selective hearing, in which the brain eliminates data it deems irrelevant in favor of the information it believes will support its preexisting worldview. By not listening to the other person, you are basically telling yourself they are bad, which will have negative effects on your relationship.

Conclusion

The first steps on your Kaizen journey may seem overwhelming, but remember what you've learned from this book: the key is to take baby steps. Our natural inclination is to cut corners and take the easy way out, but getting ahead requires putting in the time and effort. If you want to get anywhere in life, you have to learn to appreciate the little things.

Once the Kaizen process has begun, it cannot be stopped. Although it may take time for Kaizen to have a noticeable effect on your organization, it is important to collect and analyze relevant data in order to determine how effective the strategy has been. As an added bonus, you can use this data to determine which alterations were successful and which were not. If you notice that some divisions have improved while others are still struggling, you can direct your attention there. It's also possible that the staff there hasn't fully embraced the liberating power of Kaizen. No matter what, it is your job to keep advocating for change.

With Kaizen, you can expect to face many difficulties, but you must never give up. Remember that any problem can be solved by first isolating its component parts and then resolving them one by one.